Praise for *Spin the Bottle Service*

"A subtle, yet warm page-turner, *Spin the Bottle Service* uses excellent storytelling and descriptions of Paul and Kirsten's travels to help readers better understand how people shape hospitality's best practices. Read and learn!"

– Marion Russdal-Hamre and Bjørn Platou, General Manager at Decon-X International AS, Oslo, Norway

"I thoroughly enjoyed reading *Spin the Bottle Service* and smiled upon several occasions – being in the same industry for over 40 years myself, you just *can't* make these stories up. If an issue arises, you need to run to it (as opposed to away from it), truly own the problem, and solve it. Although Paul has retired from the hospitality business, you can always count on his frank and wise wisdom, no-nonsense approach, and commitment to caring – which comes through in his and Kirsten's book."

– Howard Bennett, Managing Director at Radisson Collection Hotel, Xing Guo Shanghai

"With this book, Kirsten and Paul turn their many years of experience in hospitality and travel adventures into great storytelling, leading the reader to reflect on, reconsider, and be inspired by how to balance technology and exceptional customer experiences.

"Their often humorous and down-to-earth musings, stories, and anecdotes capture you immediately as they're so easy to relate to. Although written from a hospitality point of view, the practical insights and tools offered can easily be applied by anyone – in any industry – who wishes to truly up their game on service touchpoints."

– Jan Spooren, Talent Development and Management Specialist

"A great insight and fresh take on what delivering genuine service is all about – and the importance of the human touch to excel or fail at it. Written in a straightforward way with a touch of humour, *Spin the Bottle Service* would be useful for everyone in all layers of the service industry. A nice read for starters and professionals."

– Mark Mosselman, International Hotelier

"An authentic, inspirational, and pragmatic book based on great storytelling from Paul and Kirsten, who share their service experiences from years of extensive world travels. They share their stories in an entertaining yet compelling fashion, which makes for a great read. The lessons learned are plentiful, accessible, and applicable. I particularly appreciated the approach of delivering great service based on human values rather than systems and procedures, which is truly what hospitality is all about in the end. Inspiring, entertaining, and a true reflection of the exceptional man and woman behind this book!"

– Bertrand Petyt, CEO of Ausonia Cruise Holding, Managing Partner at Vitruvius Partners Group, Professor at International University of Monaco, and member of the Board of Advisors at Long Island University

"We intuitively understand that many aspects of life and work form an energy that suffocates the most authentic kinds of people-to-people connection. As much as we would like to reduce this force of energy, we struggle to find a place to begin. Enter Paul and Kirsten. Their personal stories and wisdom not only reveal a heartfelt way to build such connection, but also help us locate an ideal place to begin again. At its essence, *Spin the Bottle Service* reflects Paul and Kirsten's kindness as the new operating system for creating and living in a kinder and gentler world."

– Joe Jacobi, Olympic Gold Medalist, Performance Coach, Executive Coach

"A well-written book from two insiders in the service industry with many good stories about their experiences as guests from a global perspective. Employees and leaders in service management will benefit from it because, with the use of many good examples followed by tasks, it describes the enormous importance the individual employee's commitment and dedication has for a hospitality business' success or mediocrity."

– Christian Gartmann, International Hotelier, Carlson Fellow, and retired Area Vice President at the predecessor to Radisson Hotel Group, Carlson Rezidor

"I loved how *Spin the Bottle Service* pulled me in with its stories about real-life experiences. Paul and Kirsten's writing is very genuine, which makes it attractive and interesting, and I enjoyed exploring the guest's point of view when they put us in the guest's shoes.

"Every topic covered is a best practice module and case study any member of the hospitality industry can reflect on and implement in their job. As a hotelier, having stories from different service fields was beneficial for me to benchmark and evaluate further. I'm sure industry members will enjoy and benefit from this book a lot."

– Erdem Bilgin, General Manager at Radisson Blu Hotel and Spa, Istanbul Tuzla

"Excellent book for hospitality students and industry leaders. *Spin the Bottle Service* is full of genuine hospitality stories and examples from Paul and Kirsten's global journey. Nothing is fake in this book. It's written in a fun and interesting way, and I love that it asks the reader to stop and reflect by asking relevant questions after each chapter. It's an inspiring collection of stories and life lessons. I will use this book in the Master of Luxury Management class at The International University of Monaco."

– Beathe-Jeanette Lunde, Hospitality Industry Expert and former Executive Vice President of Human Resources at Carlson Group USA

"With remarkable examples, Paul and Kirsten Moxness show the importance of genuine hospitality, from creating moments of truth at every customer touchpoint to keeping a make-it-right attitude. To the point: People make the difference!

"It's a fantastic and enjoyable book that should be used as food for thought by anyone who wants to start a career in the hospitality industry, as a reminder to active leaders, and as an eye-opener to anyone hoping to improve customer satisfaction."

– René M. Singeisen, Hospitality Consultant and former General Manager of international chain hotels

"If you want to get into tourism, or have already been working in it for many years, this is the book for you. It is outstanding, and its authors write in a very personal and readable style. They are clearly concerned about the true meaning of quality service, wherever in the world."

– Guillermo Ortiz-Acuna, Hotel Marketing Director, Costa Rica

"A fascinating trip, told in superb detail, through a great international career in the hotel industry. A life well-lived, a career well-shared, a great read for anyone considering a career in hotels or for well-heeled travellers interested in a peek backstage."

– David McMillan, President and CEO of Axis Hospitality International and former CEO of International Hotel and Restaurant Association

"*Spin the Bottle Service* will not only help you deliver more personalized and caring service, but it will also help you be a better guest. If Paul and Kirsten send one clear message, it is that recognizing the person on the other side of the table makes for a better life experience, regardless of which side of the table you are on. Well written, interesting, and informative."

– Maggie Craig, Award-Winning International Screenwriter and Filmmaker

Spin the Bottle Service

Hospitality in the Age of AI

by Kirsten and Paul Moxness

Published by How2Conquer
1990 Hosea L. Williams Drive NE
Atlanta, Georgia 30317
www.how2conquer.com

First edition, June 2021

Illustrations by Telia Garner
Book design by Emily Owens
Edited by Katherine Guntner

Printed in the United States of America

Library of Congress Control Number: 2021935519

Print ISBN 978-1-945783-11-1
Ebook ISBN 978-1-945783-12-8

This book is dedicated to our parents, the late
Nina and Poul Petersen, and **Pat and John Moxness**.
On opposite sides of the planet, they raised us to open
our eyes to the wonders of the world, to be open and
inquisitive, respectful, humble, and grateful for all
that we can learn and everyone we may meet.

Contents

Before We Begin... 1
About Kirsten and Paul... 1

Introduction... 3
Hospitality in the age of AI: It's the people, stupid... 3
Where does "Spin the Bottle Service" come from?... 6
Kirsten's globetrotting parents... 10
Paul's Dale Carnegie dad and service-minded mom... 11

Great Teams Make Great Experiences... 13
How to honeymoon South African style... 13
Rosemary's Restaurant: The strip mall restaurant that outperformed the best on the Strip... 17
Bushman's Kloof: A team approach to caring... 19

Communication and Understanding... 24
Helping guests navigate available options... 24
ABC: A simple communication cadence... 26
An unfortunate series of events in Norway... 29

Getting Recognition Right... 34
Tullin's Café, Oslo: Playing your song was their tune for success... 36
The River Inn, Washington, DC: Always a smile for us... 38
Skinny Duke's Glorious Emporium, Kelowna: Revisiting that '70s basement party... 41

Something Special: Freebies and Upgrades... 46
K*Rico, NYC: The best table in the house... 47
Fairmont Hotel Vancouver: Upgrade or upsell... 50
British Airways: Downgrade with an upside... 52

Navigating Cultural Differences... 56
Le Trappiste, Brussels: The brasserie that closes when tourists arrive... 59
Les Garnements, Paris: Don't ask if they'll be busy... 62
Learning to bypass bias: From Kuwait to Shanghai... 65

Fancy Doesn't Have to Mean Cold and Formal 70
Top Délice: A treat at the retreat for Brussels' elite 70
San Daniele, Brussels: Comfortable perfection 74

Franchise: Creating a Personal Touch at Scale 77
Hertz: Pink cars and the personal touch 77

Feedback and Follow-Up: Our Two Favorite F-Words 82
The Curious Café in Kelowna 84
Maxine DeHart: Ramada Hotel, Kelowna 85

Children Are Also Customers 88
Agadhoe Heights: Superstar service for a kid 89
Mandalay Bay, Las Vegas: A minor issue of underage alcohol service 91
Hyatt Regency, Huntington Beach: Three glasses to go 92

Not Picture Perfect: Resolving Problems....95
Scandinavian Airlines: A series of unforced errors.... 96
Air Canada: Above and beyond 100

When It Goes South: Safety and Crisis Management 105
When crises come calling, remember *The Martian* *106*
When the spotlight shines, don't hide in the shadows.... 110

Genuine Gratitude: The Glue That Holds It All Together....114
Job well done: Creating a culture of gratitude 114
The problem with automating gratitude 115
La Bussola Restaurant, Kelowna: Going a step further.... 116
Why is it easier to be grateful during trying times?.... 117

Start Spinning the Bottles 120
Tactical tips towards practical progress 120
Risk assessment: Where are we now?.... 120
Gaps and vulnerabilities 122
Plan of action.... 123
Making it happen 124
Engaging with expertise.... 125

Conclusion....127
Hospitality: It's the people, period. 127

Annexes 129
- Risk assessment 129
- Gaps and vulnerabilities 132
- Plan of action 133
- Engaging with expertise 134

Acknowledgements 135
- Special thanks 136
- Places we return to 136

About the Authors 140
Reading Group Discussion Questions 141

Before We Begin...

All the stories in this book come from personal experience. We've taken few literary liberties. The people and places are real. Our experiences are real. No one has paid or provided any promotional support to have their story included.

We can't say that everyone would have the same experience or perception of these people and places as we do, but the stories, lessons, and impressions are as truthful and real as we remember them.

We are forever grateful for all the places we've been. We know we are privileged.

Hospitality brings people together – together to learn from each other and better understand each other. If you're in hospitality, we hope these stories inspire you to travel, to experience, and to care. We also hope they'll inspire you to find your own way to introduce "Spin the Bottle Service," impress your guests, and turn drop-ins and walk-ins into regular returnees, promotors, advocates, and friends.

The world needs hospitality. People need hospitality. Hospitality needs people.

About Kirsten and Paul

Kirsten grew up in an active, athletic family in Denmark. Her parents travelled the world with a Danish gymnastics team in 1954. During the year they sailed the Seven Seas, they fell in love in Australia and got engaged in Sri Lanka before returning home to marry and raise their three children. In 1976, Kirsten joined a high school exchange program and enjoyed being a senior at Glenbrook South High School in Glenview, north of Chicago. The impact of that year was so powerful that she returned a few years later to explore more of the continent with a friend.

The places they saw, the people they met! The experiences of her exchange student year and follow-up visit as an intrepid explorer became the foundation upon which she built the dreams that drove her to become a successful entrepreneur in the massage and wellness industry. The company she founded in Denmark in 1993 is still successfully operating under new ownership today. She sold the business, and in 2007, Kirsten accompanied Paul when he was transferred to Belgium, where she became a sought-after massage therapist at Brussels' largest, most exclusive spa and sports club.

Paul was born in Jasper, a railroad junction *cum* tourist town, in Canada's Rocky Mountains.

In 1978, Paul graduated from high school in the then-small city of Kelowna, BC, Canada. Being a lazy kid with few ambitions, he accepted his parents' offer of a one-way ticket to Norway, where the plan was to spend a year learning the language and culture of his paternal grandfather. That gap year lasted four decades. It included a 31-year career where he started out as a night security guard in a hotel that didn't want to hire him and literally went from basement to boardroom. He was Vice President of Corporate Safety and Security for the Radisson Hotel Group when he retired from the company in 2018.

During his time with Radisson, Paul's work took him to over 60 countries around the world. Along the way, he earned a Carlson Fellows Award, the company's highest individual award for leadership, and, in the same year he retired, he was selected as IFSEC's International #1 Global Influencer in the category for Security Executives.

Introduction

Hospitality in the age of AI: It's the people, stupid

We live in an age of digitalization. When COVID-19 locked us down in 2020, we opened our digital devices and literally Zoomed into the world from wherever we were. We could talk to friends, family, colleagues, competitors, and counterparts. We could explore anything anywhere, buy anything anytime, and sell anything to anyone. With food and drink delivered, we downloaded exercise videos like yoga, Pilates, and even Jane Fonda's old aerobics routines to help keep some of us in shape – and maybe guilt those of us who couldn't find the strength to turn off Netflix.

Soon enough, our fridge app will talk to our supermarket app. We won't even have to order online anymore. The supermarket app will check our calendar app, schedule delivery when we're home (preferably not in the middle of an exciting episode of our latest show). Hopefully, the supermarket app will talk to the wine store app that will talk to our wine fridge app and ensure that the right bottle is available at the right temperature on our stay-at-home-steak-night-date-night. We can do anything from the comfort of our couches.

Almost anything, that is. During the pandemic, we couldn't travel. At least not like we used to. In many areas, we couldn't go to restaurants, bars, or clubs, and when places did open up, it was different. In some restaurants, menus were online-only, and so was ordering and payment. For hotels, booking and check-in were online, you got your key on your phone, entered your room, enjoyed your stay, and then checked out and paid online.

Some hotels even advertised that the use of mobile keys was to reduce the need for interaction with staff, so the guest would be safer during their stay. The subliminal message was that physically meeting a staff member could be harmful to your health.

Digital innovation in hotels and hospitality is here to stay, and to be honest, a lot of it is overdue and will help smooth and improve the guest experience. Still, digital innovation shouldn't become a replacement for the true traveller or guest experience.

During a Hospitality Tomorrow webinar in April 2020, Wolfgang Neumann, former CEO of the Rezidor Hotel Group (now Radisson Hotel Group), said:

> *"Our industry, at the end of the day, is all about personal experiences and human interactions."*

In other words, no matter how much digitalization may help support travel and hospitality, it's unlikely that we'll travel halfway around the world to another country and another culture just to see how their robots perform turndown service. It's also unlikely that we'll choose a restaurant solely to compare their app to the app at our usual place. To compare appetizers, maybe, but apps in the iPhone sense? We doubt it.

In hotels, restaurants, or any hospitality business – actually, in almost any business – people will still be the true differentiators. As many of the transactional portions of travel, hotel, or restaurant experiences become less personal through digitalization, our personal interactions will become even more important than they already are.

Individually, before we met, and later together, we have travelled the world. Bali, Beijing, Bangkok. Cape Town, Copenhagen, Kelowna. Vegas, Vancouver, Venice. Chicago, Shanghai, Singapore. Nyborg, New York, New Delhi. In his Christmas letter to family in Canada one year, Paul simply wrote the ABCs of places he had visited that year. Yes, there was at least one place for every letter between A (Aberdeen) and Z (Zagreb).

The Danish writer Hans Christian Andersen, he of *The Ugly Duckling* fame, once wrote: "To travel is to live." (Actually, he wrote, "At rejse er at leve," but we thought it best to translate it for you.)

We have fully experienced what he meant when he wrote those words. We've also been blessed to have had some unbelievable, top-of-the-line experiences around the world. From first-class champagne on intercontinental flights to five-star hotels to exclusive entertainment events, we've seen, felt, tasted, and tried more than we ever dreamed possible. The executive floors at the Shangri-La Bangkok. Hotel Ukraina in Moscow, both when it was a Soviet-run Hotel Intourist – where passports were confiscated until you checked out, and the phone rang every night with a husky, female voice offering "Russian girls" – and again after it became part of the Radisson Collection, with an Olympic-size pool in the underground spa and wellness area and a Bentley dealership in the lobby. The Park Hyatt Dubai, the brand-new Bellagio in Vegas, the remote Bushman's Kloof in the South African wilderness. We've seen the sights, gazed at the views, and marvelled at the awesome architecture.

Recently, while flipping through the tens of thousands of images from our travels, we suddenly realized that of all the places we had been and all the sights we had seen, only a few experiences stood out as truly exceptional. These, our most memorable moments, were fewer and farther between than we had expected. We started to think about them and what made them more special than the many special places we had been or sights we had seen.

The shoe shiners on the Istanbul ferry docks, tourist guides in Bali, and taxi drivers in Shanghai are all reminders to us of the famous quote attributed to Maya Angelou: "People will forget what you said, people will forget what you did, but people will never forget how you made them feel." We'll never forget how encounters with people we've met made us feel.

In the world of restaurants, hotels, and hospitality, there is another, simpler quote to keep in mind during these times of ever-increasing implementation of technology in day-to-day operations: "It's the people, stupid!" They're the ones who make the biggest difference, simply because of how they make people feel before, during, and after every meal, every meeting, or every stay.

The steakhouse owner in New York City. The server in Belgium. A 25-year-old chef and his mother. Two guys running a simple, bare-bones brasserie in Paris. A cadre in a strip mall restaurant. The three-star hotel with a five-star staff.

Implementing new technologies may be ever more affordable, but it's still expensive. Changing the design, layout, or menu may also briefly attract or re-attract clientele, but the novelty will wear off, and there is still a cost involved.

Hospitality businesses are already paying for the people they employ, and changing the way your team makes customers, clients, and guests feel can be as simple as a spin of the bottle. "Spin the Bottle Service" is not a game for pre-teens testing pubescent excitement. It's a way to replace the corporate standards that have become so mechanical, robotic, and repetitive that customers know the lines before they are said. For example, when, after following the orders from the restaurant computer directing them to enquire about the guest satisfaction level at table two (three minutes after the plates were plonked down), the servers turn away before the guest gives them the expected line, "It's great, thanks."

We've taken some of our most memorable moments from all over the world and created "Spin the Bottle Service" – a concept that can be adapted and adopted by any hotel, restaurant, or guest-serving business anywhere.

Where does "Spin the Bottle Service" come from?

It could come from anywhere, but we discovered "Spin the Bottle Service" when Paul transferred to Brussels, Belgium, in 2007. When we first moved, our landlord was waiting for a part to arrive for the kitchen range. We ate out every evening for over a month. Like many foreign people in foreign places, at first we stuck to the tried and tested. We consumed numerous pizzas at our neighbourhood Pizza Hut. It was right next to the Carrefour (similar to Walmart) that was close to where we lived. Our other main haunts those first few weeks were restaurants and brasseries closer to the tourist trail, where menus were always posted outside, and some of them even had pictures of the meals. Yes, we had been many places, tried and tasted many things, but this was our new hometown. For some reason, it felt best to play it safe – at least for the first week or two.

We weren't even into our third week when we met Serge. (It would take many more weeks before we learned that was his name.) About a block from the Pizza Hut was a small brasserie called Le Deauville. Hardly anyone – least of all the owner – was a fan of speaking English, but Serge liked to try out his skills, so he was almost always our server. When we tipped too much, he gave us change and told us what was appropriate. He translated the menus and, once he got to know us, suggested the specials – the ones that weren't on the menu.

One evening, when we were out after dinner and only wanted a beer, Serge happily obliged. In the trusted Belgian way, he brought two Duvel glasses and two bottles of Duvel beer on a silver tray. In Belgium, every beer has a glass and every beer is only poured into the appropriate glass. Serge poured a beer into the glass and placed it in front of Kirsten, the label facing her. He then put the bottle down on the table. The label was facing off to the side, but with a quick, almost-invisible flick of the wrist, Serge spun the bottle round, so its label too was facing Kirsten. He then poured the second bottle into the second glass and repeated the process.

We were enjoying our evening, so when our glasses were almost empty, we ordered a second round of drinks. Shortly thereafter, Serge arrived with his tray. Two new bottles. Two new glasses.

"Save the dishwashing," Paul said. "Just pour the beers into the glasses we have."

Serge looked perplexed, but somewhere along the line he had probably taken a course that taught him that "customers are always right." He looked around, almost nervously, and then poured a bottle of Duvel into Kirsten's glass. He then put the bottle on the table and gave a twist of the wrist to ensure the label was facing her. Then he did the same for Paul.

We can't remember, probably for soon-to-be-obvious reasons, what we were celebrating, but we must have been celebrating something because as our glasses neared the state of empty, we summoned Serge. "Another round, please!"

Serge smiled and headed for the bar. Soon he was back with his silver tray. It contained two bottles of Duvel and two clean Duvel glasses.

"Save the dishwashing," Paul said.

"No, this time we do it my way," Serge replied, almost apologetically. "It's okay to pour one bottle into a used glass, but never two. Normally, you should always use a clean glass." Belgians often say "normally" when they want to emphasize what is most common or usual, or even expected and correct.

Serge didn't wait for us to object or say anything. He just lifted the empty glasses off the table and replaced them with the two clean ones from his tray. Then he opened, poured, and spun the bottle in the usual fashion.

This was probably not the evening we consciously noticed "Spin the Bottle Service" as a kind of simple, thoughtful signal that shows the server cares about how you perceive the way they are caring for you and catering to your wishes. It could be that we're slow learners and needed to see the process replayed in many places before we noticed it, or it could be the simple fact that Duvel beer is 8.5% alcohol by volume.

Serge was the reason we became regulars at Le Deauville, which lies at the corner of Boulevard du Souverain and Chaussée de Wavre. Across the street was a brasserie called Le Valliance, and on a third corner was a brasserie called St. Paul.

One day, we learned from his friend the bartender that Serge was no longer working at Le Deauville. Shortly thereafter, we were no longer regulars at Le Deauville. We tried Le Valliance and St. Paul, and both were fine in their own way, but we didn't become regulars at either. We missed Serge.

Several months later, we were still not regulars anywhere. We didn't go to any of the restaurants near "our Carrefour" anymore. We tried a few in the city centre. We tried some closer to home. Many of the small, simple brasseries we went to were more than adequate. The food was good, the wine was good, the beer was good. We were spoiled for choice. So we kept choosing and didn't become regulars anywhere.

One evening we stepped into La Terrasse, at Merode, on the corner of Avenue du Tervueren and Avenue des Celtes. There he was! Serge!

"Where have you been?" we asked.

"Right here, waiting for you," he replied.

We became regulars at La Terrasse.

Over a short period, we noticed something. We had been there once or twice before, and both times it had been half empty. It was also half empty the night we had our reunion with Serge. But as time passed, the restaurant was fuller and fuller. The clientele was happier, the food became better, and the restaurant was clearly more successful.

So successful that one evening when we walked in, it was packed. To our dismay, every single table was occupied. Except one. It had a reserved sign on it. Serge was busy behind the bar, helping the bartender while wiping sweat from his brow.

As we turned to leave, struggling to decide which of the other three brasseries close by we should try, we heard a familiar voice shout out.

"Hey, where are you going?"

Like the well-brought-up Canadian his mother wishes Paul were, he started with an apology.

"Sorry," he said. "We should have booked."

"No, please stay," said Serge. "You can have this table," he said, pointing at the table that had a prime place right next to the windows along Avenue des Celtes.

"It's reserved," Paul said.

"Yes!" Serge excitedly exclaimed. "Reserved for you."

When things quieted down that evening, Serge explained that every day upon opening, he placed reserved signs on the best tables in the restaurant. There were a lot of regulars. He didn't want to disappoint them if they hadn't booked and the restaurant was busy. It usually worked out pretty well, he said. His tip to us was that if we came as a couple, he would always find a table for us. If we were more than two, he would appreciate a reservation.

For a good while, everyone who visited us in Brussels was taken to La Terrasse – Kirsten's mother, the minister that married us, Kirsten's friends from one of her former workplaces.

Then one day, Serge disappeared again. During our decade in Brussels, we never did find him again, but for a while, we did our best. La Terrasse wasn't the same without him. By the time we stopped going there, it wasn't as busy without him either.

Although we never saw him again, we still have many memories of Serge, the server who first introduced us to "Spin the Bottle Service."

Before we go any further, let's fill you in on how our backgrounds drove us towards the world of service and hospitality.

Kirsten's globetrotting parents

Erik Flensted-Jensen was the founder and leader of "The Danish Gym Team," a troop of young gymnasts that toured the world on up to year-long voyages between the 1940s and 1980s. In 1954, Nina Marie Swartz was the leader of the women's troop and Poul Willum Petersen was the flag bearer for the men. That year the troop sailed from Denmark as far south as Australia and New Zealand, with stops on South Pacific islands and the Indian sub-continent, amongst many others. They didn't know each other when they set sail, but while gazing at the sun setting behind the Blue Mountains in Australia, Nina and Poul fell in love. They got engaged when they reached Colombo in Ceylon (now Sri Lanka) and, once back home in Denmark, they were married. Kirsten is their firstborn.

Growing up in the 1960s, Kirsten and her brother and sister were often told stories of the epic adventures Nina and Poul had during their year of sailing the high seas and bringing Danish culture and gymnastics shows to people on the other side of the world.

Nina and Poul were both teachers. For 44 years, Nina worked at Haslev Udvidede Højskole (HUH), a kind of gap year school that is found in Denmark and Norway. Twice per year, new groups of students in their late teens and early twenties from all over

Denmark, as well as international youth, arrived in Haslev, south of Copenhagen. They spent five months studying subjects without the pressures of exams while learning to live away from home and, for the international students, learning a new language and culture.

During Kirsten's formative years, she spent as much time at HUH as she did at home or school. Learning from her mother and father, and being part of a school community where people came from different backgrounds and nationalities, Kirsten was exposed to a broader worldview than probably many Danish children growing up in the '60s and '70s were privileged to experience.

Kirsten's mother was like a mother to every youth who came to the school. In the small town of Haslev, everyone knew Nina and Poul. They were the people you could always turn to, and theirs was the home where you were always welcome.

This atmosphere of hospitality, trust, and caring was something Kirsten naturally took with her when she started her own business in relaxation and massage therapy, and for fourteen years before moving to Brussels, she had everyone from leading lawyers to government ministers to famous musicians in the palms of her hands.

Paul's Dale Carnegie dad and service-minded mom

Paul's dad was a pharmacist, but he filled more than prescriptions. Sometimes he had his own drugstore, sometimes he worked for others, and sometimes he didn't work as a pharmacist at all, but service was always at the forefront of everything he did.

There always seemed to be more elderly customers that spoke little English wherever he worked. He often walked to work, and some days when Paul picked him up, there would be two or three stops on the way home to deliver prescriptions to people. They had struggled to make it to the pharmacy to drop their prescriptions off, so Paul's dad wanted to spare them the extra effort of having to come in to pick up their medications when they were ready.

When Japanese tourists started arriving in Kelowna, B.C., where Paul grew up, his dad hired youth from Japanese-Canadian families to work during their summer holidays. Some days the line at the makeup counter was long, with most people wanting restaurant recommendations rather than eyeliner tips.

Paul's mom also worked in retail, so stories around the dinner table were always about the fact that customers came first, no task was too menial, and, no matter what your job description was, if it had to do with your place of work, it was your job to ensure that it got done properly and with customer satisfaction.

Both of Paul's parents believed that every person should be treated and served with the same care and attention; that was another fact of life often repeated during those daily dinner discussions. That was also the foundation that made it possible for Paul's unexpected basement-to-boardroom career.

Every person is different, so working in service trying to please every customer can be challenging. Pay isn't often great and working weekends and long hours doesn't appeal to everyone. Paul's mom wanted her three sons to grow up to become doctors, dentists, or lawyers. Instead, Paul chose a path that led him to work in a service industry, albeit one with even longer hours and, on the face of it, one where customer interaction was always preceded by a negative experience.

What have you learned? What can you do?	
1	Serge was a server. He was also a salesman, an educator, and a professional.
2	Everyone can be like Serge.
3	Little things you do might seem to go unnoticed, but trust us, they're noticed.
➤ Think about your most recent restaurant visit. If you experienced "Spin the Bottle Service," what was it? If not, what was missing?	

Great Teams Make Great Experiences

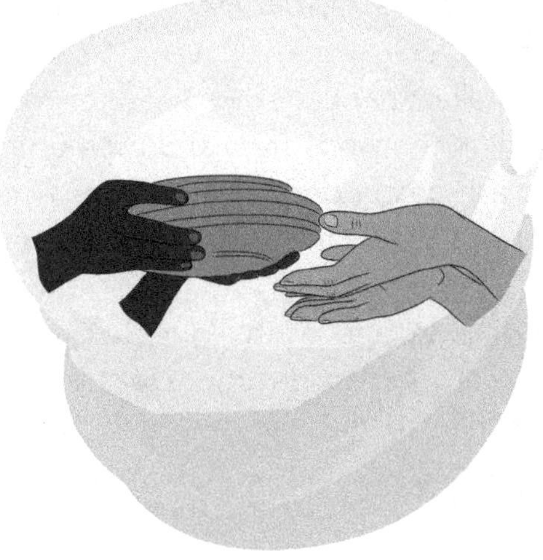

How to honeymoon South African style

We met January 5, 2000, just as the new millennium was getting underway. Two years and a few months later, we were married. Our three-week honeymoon was the only time during his career that Paul's phone was switched off for more than a few hours at a time. Actually, it wasn't switched off; it was redirected to his deputy. That was one of our best wedding presents! (Thanks, Kjell.)

We wanted our honeymoon to be an epic holiday. Paul wanted to surprise Kirsten by planning a ten-stop, four-continent, round-the-world journey. Yes, some of his ideas are best left inside his head, and this was one of those. Fortunately, a man named Dean helped steer Paul clear of what could have been an exhausting disaster of a honeymoon.

Paul had found a website offering round-the-world flights and packages. It was just an aggregator site that guaranteed that after entering your details and desires, you would receive offers from at least ten travel agents within 24 hours.

Minutes after typing in his wish list of dates and destinations, Paul received an email with the simple subject line: "Are you crazy?" The brief email begged Paul to reconsider his plan to circumnavigate the globe and spend the three weeks in South Africa instead.

What followed was a month or two of correspondence. The South African tour organizer had a very simple business model. Tell me what you want to see, when you want to see it, and what your budget is – I will make it happen. If you have a limited budget, you will sleep in a tent in the wilderness and carry and cook your own food. If you have a large budget, you will stay in five-star hotels and resorts, and your every want and need will be catered to by caring hosts and their teams.

We emailed back and forth. Much of what we were told seemed almost too good to be true. Dean provided references and they praised him to the heavens. Everything everyone had experienced had exceeded their wildest dreams of what a holiday could contain.

Paul's job was security, intelligence, crisis, and risk management. He's a natural skeptic who is always checking facts and evaluating risks. The proposals we were receiving had two obvious risk factors: 1) Everything had to be paid up front, and 2) the company was not registered with the South African Tourism Organization.

Rather than trust the company, Paul started to investigate. Via sites like VirtualTourist.com (remember them?) and others, he sought out customers who had used the company, found their contact details, and asked for a reference. Everyone responded that everything had been perfect. "Trust Dean and his company," they said. "You will have the trip of a lifetime."

But paying a large sum of money in advance to an African company that wasn't registered with their official tourism organization still set off alarm bells in Paul's mind. Through company contacts in Cape Town, he was able to get the email address for the CEO of South Africa's tourism board. The CEO responded that although they normally wouldn't endorse a non-member, he considered Dean to be a personal friend and one of the best tourism ambassadors the country had. He only wished Dean's company would join their organization.

A few days later, Paul received an email from Dean. "Make up your mind," it said. "You've contacted the government and every bloody person who ever booked with us. Either trust us or don't, but book now or quit stalling and contacting all these people."

Shortly thereafter, the check was in the mail.

The plan we were given sounded awesome. On arrival in Johannesburg, we would be met by a qualified driver and guide. The guide would take us to a guest house on the outskirts of Kruger National Park for our first night. We would then spend a day or two at a resort in the park, where we would be guaranteed to see the Big Five (lions, leopards, rhinos, elephants, and buffalo). Once that was ticked off, we would move to more remote spots where big game wasn't guaranteed, but relaxation and natural beauty were. Our stays would become even more remote after our guide and driver handed us off at a secluded resort near the East Coast. An even more remote resort would collect us there and take us to their beachfront property, which was made up of treehouses in the jungle. It was ecotourism before that became a thing. Only a limited number of people were allowed in the vast area per night, so this was a place we could completely relax without cell phone service or other disruptions. From there, a small plane would collect us and we'd fly to Durban to enjoy a couple of urban nights overlooking the Indian Ocean before our experience ended and we'd fly home, which at the time was Copenhagen. For the price we paid, we were told everything was included except wine and souvenirs.

Despite all the background checks and reassurances, there was still an air of apprehension as we cleared customs and entered the arrivals hall at Oliver Tambo International Airport in Johannesburg. Would anyone be waiting for us, or had we just forked over our whole honeymoon budget only to be stuck in a faraway land with no backup plan?

Any fear we had quickly subsided. Our guide's name was Keith. He was in his mid-fifties and a retired police officer. He took us to the van that would be our transport for the first nine days of our South African adventure.

En route to our first stop, Keith said he was going to pull in to fill the petrol tank, and he suggested we grab some lunch and coffee before we headed to the guest house where we'd spend the night.

As he filled the tank, we went into the café. Keith joined us and we enjoyed a sandwich and coffee. When the bill arrived, we reached for it and our wallet. Keith was shocked. "Didn't Dean tell you everything was paid for?" Keith asked. "When Dean says everything, he means everything!"

Just as the many people we had contacted had promised us, our honeymoon was an epic experience. We saw the Big Five. We got used to the early wake-up calls on crisp, cool mornings, warming cups of rooibos tea before sunrise, and pre-breakfast safari walks. We got used to driving to remote spots in the wilderness for sundowners, a kind of twilight happy hour watching the sunset in the wilderness, and we got used to some of the best food and wine we've tasted.

Except for the resort in Kruger National Park, where we ticked off the Big Five on our South African list of "must-sees," most of the places we stayed were small and run by families or local groups. At some of them, we were the only foreigners. Other guests were from Johannesburg, Cape Town, or Durban, taking advantage of reduced rates for locals at superb resorts a bit off the path beaten by European and American tourists.

Since the resorts were small and family owned, the people in charge had time for every guest either during meals or around the campfire in the evening. More than one of them told us how happy they always were when Dean made a booking. "He always pays upfront," they said. "We spend a lot of time and effort chasing payments from larger tour operators."

As our time in paradise was winding down, we found ourselves on a grassy airstrip in the middle of nowhere near the Mozambican border. A twin-engine plane arrived and flew us to a small airport outside of Durban, where a driver was supposed to meet us. There was no one there. No driver and hardly anyone in the building that was far too small to call a terminal. The people we spoke with told us not to worry, our driver was probably just stuck in traffic. About 10 minutes later, a scruffy-looking fellow wandered in with a beard that reached halfway down his chest.

"Hey, Kirsten and Paul! I'm Dean!" He certainly didn't resemble the clean-shaven man on the company website. He apologized that his driver had been delayed, and when he'd noticed our flight would be arriving early, he'd cancelled the driver, jumped in his little sedan, and headed down to meet us in person. "Sorry, it's not the driver who was late; it was me! Thought I could make it."

He asked if we'd like to see his office and a bit of the city before he took us to the hotel. His office was a small shed in the backyard of his mother's modest home in the Durban suburbs. Before digitalization had taken over travel, the company was running a very successful, internet-only business from a garden shed.

Dean was ahead of his time, and he was successful for all the reasons good hospitality people are. He was ethical, and that showed in the way he cared. He cared about his clients. He cared about the people who owned and worked at the places he booked. He cared about his country. Dean was perhaps one of the reasons we chose "Always Care" as our company name.

Rosemary's Restaurant: The strip mall restaurant that outperformed the best on the Strip

One of our trips to Las Vegas for a corporate conference coincided with Kirsten's birthday. It's not always easy to combine business and pleasure in travel, and when there is a special occasion that could be disrupted, it increases the challenge.

Paul wanted to find the best restaurant possible (i.e., affordable) for the occasion, but he was worried that with all of his company colleagues around, we would bump into someone from the office and ruin the romance of the celebratory evening. Luckily, his problems were solved as soon as he started his search: the name Rosemary's Restaurant kept popping up, and the map showed him it was located in a strip mall well off the Strip (with a capital S), which is all many visitors ever see of Las Vegas.

The plan was kept secret from Kirsten. The taxi driver who picked us up at The Bellagio had heard of the restaurant and "kind of" knew where it was. We headed off in what he thought was the right direction, and after he'd radioed with his dispatcher a few times, we pulled into a very dimly lit parking lot. A couple of the stores were boarded up and the rest were closed for the day, but there was a little light coming from Rosemary's Restaurant. You couldn't see into the restaurant from the parking lot.

Some people say the first impression is everything. If our first impression from the parking lot wasn't exceptional, our second impression when we opened the door wasn't any better. We entered a small, cramped bar with Nevada cowboys occupying every seat and a busy young bartender pouring their drinks. A hostess asked if we had reservations for the restaurant. We confirmed, and she said, "Follow me."

Third time's the charm they say, and thankfully our third impression was much better than the first two.

We were seated in a very romantic, quiet corner of the restaurant. When he arrived, our waiter knew it was Kirsten's birthday, and we were off to a much better start than we had feared when the cab pulled into the parking lot outside.

After explaining the menu, the waiter said he would fetch the sommelier. He wouldn't want to help us choose wine on a special occasion.

The sommelier looked like he was hardly of legal drinking age, but he seemed to know his stuff. We aren't wine experts, so we do appreciate it when a server or sommelier can help us find something nice. The good ones do that, while the poorer ones try to maximize margins and profits without the customer catching on. (Note to all: the customer usually catches on.)

Our sommelier was a good one. He asked us what we liked. He asked us where we were from. He didn't ask why we were there, because he already knew it was Kirsten's birthday. When he heard Paul had grown up in British Columbia, he apologized for not having BC wine on the menu, but knowing that we were leaning towards the lamb, he suggested a wine from Washington state. "That's as close to local as we can get for you," he said. It was exquisite and paired perfectly with the lamb we had for dinner.

We could see the entire restaurant from our corner table, and we noticed how the servers, sommelier, and hosts worked together to create an incredibly smooth, seamless service at every table. Every table had "their" server, but there was no rule that said every server couldn't assist any table. Nothing was rushed, yet no one seemed to have to wait for anything. One of the most impressive, almost-undetectable things we saw was something we decided to call Rosemary's Statue of Liberty Play.

A group of eight or ten people were enjoying their evening at a table not too far from ours. When the server was collecting their plates after the main course, one of the guests at the table had a question. The server leaned down to chat with the elderly guest, and as he did so, the hand in which he was holding the three or four plates he had already collected rotated so the plates were behind him. Within seconds, one of his colleagues had taken those plates and proceeded to remove the remaining plates from the table. Both the conversation the server had with the guest and the table clearing continued uninterrupted.

Great service can be as easy as a simple spin of the bottle, but when teams perform like they did in Rosemary's Restaurant, great service takes on a whole new dimension.

Bushman's Kloof: A team approach to caring

Seven years after our honeymoon and a year before South Africa hosted the World Cup of Soccer in 2010, we had a second opportunity to visit the wonderful country at the southern tip of the African continent.

Paul was busy helping prepare hotels for the largest international event South Africa had ever hosted, and he was busy collaborating with other local and global corporate security leaders to help ensure the soccer spectacle would be safe, secure, and successful for all.

In September 2009, we had the opportunity to tack a week of holiday onto one of Paul's trips to Cape Town. Again, we turned to Dean for guidance on what to see and do on the West Coast of the country. Again, he surprised us by suggesting something we never would have considered. "Go to Bushman's Kloof," he said. "It's in the middle of nowhere – there's no beach, no big game, no real mountains. You'll love it."

We looked at the map. Yup, it was indeed in the middle of nowhere. We would spend the better part of a week at a place that seemed to have hardly anything going for it. No beach, no waterfalls, no lake. No nothing. But, like most of Dean's previous clients, we'd become ambassadors and recommended his company to anyone and everyone we knew who planned trips to the country. We trusted him, so we said yes to his proposal of sending us off into the great unknown.

Before we left Cape Town, Dean called us to let us know Bushman's Kloof had been selected as the 2009 resort of the year by a major global travel publication. "Had I known that was coming, I could have charged you double!" he joked.

Bushman's Kloof is a wilderness reserve a few hours' drive north of Cape Town if you take Highway 7. The last stretch is an hour of gradually narrowing, deteriorating road from the township of Clanwilliam to the gates of the reserve.

We had rented a car and before we set off, we contacted Bushman's Kloof as agreed in our correspondence with them. "Follow our instructions carefully," they said. "Drive to Clanwilliam. Have lunch and fill petrol there. Before you leave Clanwilliam, call us again. That way, if you don't show up in a reasonable amount of time, we'll come to look for you. There is no cell service between Clanwilliam and the resort, so if you get lost or stuck, you'll want to know we'll be coming for you."

Clanwilliam is a small town about 200 km north of Cape Town. It's not especially picturesque – just a quiet, dusty town. Like most places we've visited in South Africa, people were quiet but friendly and hospitable. We had a sandwich and water for lunch on the hot, sunny afternoon before filling the car with petrol. We called the resort as requested and then set off.

Shortly outside of town, the asphalt was replaced by gravel, and not much farther along, the gravel was gone, and we were driving along a dirt road. Paul was constantly reminding himself to stay on the right side of the road, which in South Africa is the left side of the road. It didn't matter much though; we can't remember meeting a single car as we drove along the snake-like road that wound its way through the countryside. Just as we were beginning to think we must have missed the turnoff, we saw a sight we couldn't miss: the gates at Bushman's Kloof. The tall, bright white concrete walls were separated by shiny, black wrought iron gates, and there was an intercom on the left-hand side of the wall.

"Great! You're here," the voice that answered the intercom said. "Or, at least, you will be here in about twenty minutes."

The welcoming committee was waiting when we arrived. The managers, the young man who would be our guide, a receptionist, a bellman, and a housekeeper were all lined up outside the main building. The bellman and the guide took our car keys, and the others took us inside. We were given a welcome drink to sip as we completed the registration formalities.

The guide returned and took us to our accommodation. When we saw our bungalow, it was picture-postcard perfect. For once, reality was even better than the brochure.

By the end of our first evening, the bartender knew our names and drink preferences. At breakfast the next morning, the staff already knew our names. We were in the shoulder season, so the resort wasn't fully booked. The only other non-South Africans were an American couple and their daughter, who was about to start a year on an exchange program at the University of Cape Town.

Our guide had a heavy Afrikaans accent and a deep knowledge of the geography, wildlife, and history of his surroundings. Like many young South Africans, he had a yearning to travel and hoped he could one day be in our shoes, experiencing the world instead of only sharing an experience of his world.

Bushman's Kloof remains one of the most memorable, romantic, and relaxing places we've ever had the opportunity to stay. Despite the lack of obvious attractions other places advertise, they welcome you into their world of wide-open spaces with high-quality accommodations, food and drink, and a wonderful staff that is trained to treat every guest like they're a family friend. It was the kind of place where we arrived almost wondering what we'd do to pass the time there for a whole week and where departure day came far too soon.

At breakfast on checkout day, we were told to leave all our belongings in the guest room. After settling the bill and bidding our hosts farewell, we emerged to find a squeaky-clean car (inside and out) packed with our belongings and two bottles of chilled water in the cup holders. We almost didn't recognize it as ours. It was cleaner than when we had picked it up at the rental counter in Cape Town.

"Call us from Clanwilliam!" were the final words from the welcome team, who'd now become the departure team, as they waved us off.

Dean had done it again for us – he'd chosen a place that cared as much about their hospitality as he did. We never booked with Dean again. He died not too long after our last visit to South Africa. We're confident though that whether on big game reserves, on the beachfront, or in the wilderness like Bushman's Kloof, the hospitality he introduced us to lives on through the people who took care of us because they continue to care about their guests, their properties, and the world around them.

What have you learned? What can you do?	
1	Great service is more important than a great location.
2	Great teams trust each other for support.
3	Overall results improve when teams work towards a common goal.
4	A good salesperson represents more than just their product or their company. Dean represented South Africa.
5	Hospitality leaders step up when service struggles. Dean personally picked us up when the driver was delayed.
6	Proactive customer care amplifies guest experience, and customer care extends beyond your perimeter.
7	All-inclusive is all-inclusive. Add-ons and fees are frustrating.
➤ How can you make teams better where you work?	

Communication and Understanding

If great experiences start with great teams, the next key building block is communication. In today's world, where everything is online, communication can appear complicated and nigh on impossible when one watches how fast conversations on social media can spiral out of control.

The days of spinning stories to make them look nice are long gone, but there are still ways to set up a framework that can reduce confusion, avoid misunderstandings, and use empathy and care to build back trust when things go wrong.

In this section, we'll look at one way to help guests wish for services you can provide. We'll also look at a simple system of step-by-step communication for resolving problems when they arise and show how it can, along with heartfelt empathy, turn guest feelings of fear and frustration into gratitude and a memorable experience.

Helping guests navigate available options

Back in the '90s, before online booking became widely available, Paul spent a few months helping run the reservations department for three hotels in the same city. To increase efficiency and optimize the use and yield of the rooms they had available, the company had chosen to centralize the reservations department. A guest could call one number, and the reservations agents, who had oversight of all three hotels, could help place the guest in the most appropriate room in the most appropriate hotel at the most appropriate rate.

At least that was the theory.

Reality had proven a bit more challenging. Agents were biased towards "their" hotels. They had difficulty promoting hotels equally, and they had difficulty selling suites when the city was heavily booked, which was every day from Monday through Thursday. Paul was brought in to analyze why this was the case and help improve both the results and the employee satisfaction rate, which had taken a dramatic dive following the changes.

He didn't know much about how to run a reservations department, but he was a pretty good listener and the team had some useful suggestions on how things might be improved. He also brought in a colleague who had worked in a bigger, busier city to help show the local associates how to sell expensive suites and rooms at proper price points.

One of the most helpful solutions, however, came shortly after Paul arrived in the city and was having dinner in a local restaurant. In Norway, potatoes accompany almost every evening meal. In some restaurants, you choose how you prefer your potatoes: fries, boiled, baked, etc.

When taking his order, the server asked, "What kind of potatoes would you like?"

"Baked, please," said Paul.

"We don't have that," said the server. She waited for his next answer without offering any suggestion as to what they did have. That switched on a light in Paul's head.

One of the issues the hotel reservations team had was that on busy days, they quickly sold out of standard single rooms. When guests called and asked to make a reservation on a day when the standard rooms had already been sold, they weren't informed of what their limited choices were. This often led to the agents just adding to the overbooking issue that the front desk would have to deal with later. Premium rooms went unsold but were filled with guests from the overbooked standard rooms.

The team was trained to sell the premium rooms when standard rooms were sold out by offering them like choices on a menu.

"We have business class, junior suites, or one-bedroom suites. Which would you prefer?"

Some guests questioned this, but the team was surprised at how many didn't and just picked from the menu that was offered. Guests who did question the menu were informed that more choices and lower rates were likely to be available if they booked in advance.

Two things happened. Booking lead times increased, which helped the hotels better manage their operational staffing levels, and the average room rate increased because guests were paying for upgrades, rather than receiving them as free upgrades simply because the hotel had oversold standard rooms.

One thing didn't happen. Guest satisfaction, including their views on the booking process, did not decrease. The team had been worried that guests would be upset at having to pay a higher rate. Most were businesspeople though, so they understood, and those that needed – or wanted – lower rates started to call further in advance.

Choice is a funny thing. When given a list of possibilities, most people are more than happy to choose from the list. Some will ask for exceptions; accepting them is dependent on the capability of the supplier.

After all, it's why restaurants have menus instead of just asking patrons what they want to eat.

ABC: A simple communication cadence

When Paul started his career, immersion training was immense. There were several days of learning the ways of the company, learning about the property and its guest service offerings, and learning what behaviours were expected and required from every employee. That included the lowly security guards who were mainly hidden away in a basement office until problems arose.

In 1995, the company Paul worked for became a master franchise partner for Radisson Hotels, based in the US. Many travellers are unaware of the fact that although hotels carry a big brand sign on their door, they may or may not have big brand backing and support, especially in areas like safety and security.

Often there is a standard of service or operation that applies to every property, but how detailed it is varies greatly. For safety and security, it might be limited to saying the hotel needs to provide good safety and security by following all applicable laws and regulations.

One thing that was mandatory for all hotels joining the Radisson portfolio in 1995, even as franchises, was that every employee had to undergo a service training program that was called (and trademarked) "Yes I Can!" Paul was in a selected group of employees chosen to attend a week-long "train the trainer" program designed both to introduce European hotels to the program and to suggest adaptations to the material that would make it more understandable and a better "fit" for European hospitality culture.

Taking this step, rather than sending corporate trainers over from the US to conduct the training program in Europe, was a good move since, as it turned out, a good deal of "cultural adjustment" was deemed necessary before the program could be rolled out in the hotels. The difference was so great that during the very first lunch break on the very first day, representatives from one of the countries threatened to walk out and return home because the course was "too American." (This may help some readers better understand the intricacies of European Union negotiations, but that's not what this book is about.)

Even in a global world, where there are definite divisions between countries and cultures on the perception of what is "normal" or "right," there are many more things that can cross boundaries with minimal challenges or changes. After travelling the world for so many years, we've concluded that people are people. We're far more alike than not, despite our bias and our prejudice.

The Yes I Can! program as it was in 1995 had a very simple, easy-to-remember approach to problem solving. It was called "ABC: Apologize, Be Understanding, Correct the Problem."

In the simple case where someone checks in to a hotel, goes up to their room, and can't switch the TV on because the batteries have been stolen from the remote control, the approach would be something like, "I'm sorry, Ms./Mr. Guest. I can understand your frustration. We'll be up with new batteries for you right away."

Sometimes, issues aren't simply resolved. The Yes I Can! program continued down the alphabet with DEF. Roughly paraphrased, that was short for "Discuss alternatives, Explain what will happen, Follow up to ensure satisfaction."

If, in the first example, it turned out that putting batteries in the remote control didn't help, support would continue along the lines of "We can try a new remote control, we can switch out the television, or we can put you in a room where the TV works." After discussing which alternative was best for the guest, or perhaps which one was most acceptable for both guest and hotel, that would be done. Assuming that resolved the issue, the employee would follow up to ensure that the issue was and remained resolved.

This approach turned out to be very effective in many of the little issues that cropped up from time to time. Apologizing and expressing empathy showed the guest that they were being listened to. Correcting the problem, discussing options, explaining actions, and following up showed commitment to ensuring that the guest was happy with how the issue was resolved.

Of course, there will always be issues that are beyond the power of a single employee. When our flight to San Francisco was cancelled, that impacted over 200 other passengers and was likely overwhelming for guest services staff, who couldn't just bring in a new plane and fly everyone to their desired destination.

Showing care, concern, and empathy does help calm most people. Even where there are a few who seem impossible to please, you'll often find that the better and more sincerely the ABCs and DEFs are executed, the fewer and farther between each "impossible" customer becomes.

Yes I Can! was also a signal to employees that they were personally empowered to provide guests with top-notch hospitality. Like many of the good service examples we shared earlier, taking a personal approach to problem-solving can also help turn a bad experience into an overall positive one and – as Paul once experienced – a potential customer complaint into a public letter of thanks to the company CEO.

An unfortunate series of events in Norway

When Paul was working as a security guard, summer was the worst time of the year. Yes, the fights and drama that accompanied Christmas party season, the supporter battles between rival fans on Cup final weekend, and the long hours of waiting during state visits with ever-changing schedules were all challenging. But summer, when everyone else was at the beach, could be a nightmare. That was especially true when the travelling teams of thieves and pickpockets arrived alongside the groups of elderly foreigners who thought Norway was crime-free.

Imagine visiting a foreign land for the first time. Just as you check in, an invisible perpetrator swipes your carry-on off the floor and disappears with hardly a trace. Your bag contained your money, your passports, and your tickets (in the old days, tickets were an important part of travel – as in no ticket, no travel). People who experienced this often reacted as if they would perish in poverty in this foreign country that looked so good in the brochure, but had turned into the scariest, most inhospitable place on Earth within moments of their arrival.

Some scoffed at the "stupid" tourist, who was so negligent and didn't take care of their belongings, and that didn't help the poor guest. It could have led to a rather long, less-than-honest but very poor review on Tripadvisor about how dangerous the hotel was and how little the staff cared.

Paul's background in psychology, and perhaps the fact that he had once watched a bus drive off with all of his worldly belongings, helped him empathize with guests who were victims of theft.

If you put yourself in their position, it was understandable that they really did feel like they would die of starvation. They had no money, so they couldn't pay for food or shelter. Even if someone gave them money, they couldn't travel because they had no passport. In the immediate trauma of discovering their loss, some seemed inconsolable.

A and B from the ABCs were helpful. Guiding people to a quiet area away from the lobby was also helpful. It was hard for them to focus as they continuously scoured the scene, like some people who repeatedly look at lottery numbers in the hopes that by some miracle, everything will change for the better.

A trauma can wipe out people's self-confidence in a flash. These guests knew they should have taken better care of their belongings. They knew they should have kept tickets, passports, and wallets on their person and not stuffed into a bag they left lying on the couch beside them while they relaxed after a long flight. They didn't need a smart aleck security guard a third their age to remind them of this.

The security team was trained to apologize that this unfortunate event happened in the hotel and show empathy and understanding for the guest's predicament. They couldn't just wave a wand and make the belongings reappear, but they could start to reassure and help the guest regain and rebuild some of their confidence.

To start with, they would ask questions the guest could answer correctly with relative ease: What is your name? Where are you from? Are you travelling in a group?

If a guest had credit cards, that was a big plus. The team could call the credit card company, but only the card owner could speak to the agent who answered. It was a few further steps along the way to building up the guest's comfort and confidence because many of the questions were again easy for the guest to answer. They could feel that progress was being made, and often this was confirmed with a "Don't worry, we'll cancel the card and send you a new one" from the card company. It was like the proverbial appearance of light at the end of the tunnel.

While the guest was on the phone with the card company (or companies, as often was the case), security would call the guest's embassy, where a relationship and rapport had been built and where they often had direct line numbers to the appropriate consular office, to inform them that one of their citizens would be coming in needing assistance with getting an emergency passport or travel document.

By the time these calls were over, and the guest had had a coffee or soft drink, life was usually looking much better. After a guided trip to the local police to get the case registered and a document that could be used for insurance and passport renewal purposes, most guests accepted the blame for the theft themselves and thanked the hotel for support. Some didn't, but most, in fact, did.

Of course, the hotel did investigate. In those days video was black and white and grainy. Stored on VHS tapes that were changed every 24 hours, but often used hundreds of times before new ones were brought into the rotation, the quality was always an issue. There was no colour, no night vision, and no HDR for backlighting. Thus weather and time of day played a vital role in determining the quality of the images. Even though the chance of finding everything intact was slim, the security team did their best. They examined the video and checked waste bins on the surrounding streets and in nearby parks. They followed up with city and police lost-and-found services.

Sometimes, persistence paid off. A seasoned business traveller from England once left the hotel in a cab to attend meetings in the city. When he stepped out of the taxi, he realized his briefcase was gone. He'd called the taxi company; they had contacted the driver, but there was no briefcase in the vehicle. He called the hotel and said it must have been left in the lobby.

This was during high season for pickpockets and lobby thieves. There was no briefcase lying around in the lobby. The video was examined and, fortunately, thanks to overcast and rather gloomy weather, the lighting was perfect for the grainy images to show that not only had the guest left the hotel with briefcase in hand, security could also see that he entered the taxi with the briefcase still in his possession.

Rather than call the guest and explain this, security called the taxi company. They contacted the driver who again said he'd checked, but there was no briefcase in the back seat. Security then called the police, explained the story, and mentioned what they could see on the video. The hotel had an excellent rapport with the police, who sent a patrol to stop the cab. It turned out that the guest had placed the small briefcase on the floor, and it had slid up under the passenger seat of the cab, so the driver, who had just looked over his shoulder into the back seat, hadn't seen it. The police brought it to the hotel, the guest was informed, and he was so happy he wrote a letter to the CEO of the airline that owned the company.

That kind of service, especially from a department that wasn't usually in the front lines of guest relations, was unheard of, he wrote. He also wrote that he was extra happy that it was security, known for their ability to work discreetly and keep secrets, that had helped him. The reason for this was that they had promised not to tell anyone about how the incident had played out, since he would soon be on vacation with his extended family. If his mother-in-law ever found out about what had happened, he would never hear the end of it, he said.

Problems will arise. Most of them can be relatively simply solved in a few steps by a trained, understanding, and empathetic staff. Some are more challenging, but taking personal responsibility to discuss, evaluate, and explain options, alongside dogged determination and follow-up, will often lead to sometimes surprising solutions and long-term loyalty from the guest whose first words to you were something along the lines of "I have a problem and it's all your fault."

What have you learned? What can you do?	
1	There's a reason why restaurants don't give customers a blank slate.
2	When offered choices from a list, most people will happily choose from it.
3	Adapting the list of choices to what you want or need to sell improves results.
➤ Think about how you offer choices. How can you use them to improve satisfaction and revenue?	

Getting Recognition Right

Computerized calendars and loyalty program management systems help us keep track of where we need to be and when we need to be there. In hospitality businesses, they help us keep track of who's coming, when they're coming, and how often they've visited us before.

In many ways, that should enable us to truly personalize guest experiences. Why, then, does it so often feel less than personal when loyalty programs spam us with offers that really show they have no idea who we are, and why do we so often notice that restaurants haven't read the remarks they asked us for in their online reservation form.

Personalizing recognition is extremely powerful. With thoughtful leadership and a well-trained team, it's also one of the most effective marketing tools available. Let's look at two examples of how recognition works, both on its own and in combination with good guest management systems.

As Paul's career grew and his title changed from Coordinator to Manager to Director to Vice President at the hotel company, the rooms we stayed in became larger, and upgrades and suites became almost commonplace. More often than not, the upgrade was accompanied by a welcome note and sometimes a small room gift – a bottle of water, a box of chocolates, some baked goods from the kitchen, and even the occasional bottle of wine. It was always a nice surprise.

Having worked on the operational side of hotels for many years, Paul was accustomed to the routine review hotels undertake of the expected arrivals lists. When he was Duty Manager, one of his tasks was to approve the reviewed list of names and which of the various types of room gifts the guest should find in the room upon arrival. It was also the Duty Manager's task to write the note that would be placed in the room with the gift.

In the good old days, when both room service and guest services were fully staffed, you could even send up a bottle of chilled champagne on ice to top-tier guests who arrived at midnight. We don't know how many of those late-arriving, unaccompanied business travellers would drink an entire bottle of champagne before their 6:00 a.m. wake-up calls, but if some did, we didn't judge them for it.

Slowly but surely, computerization of hotel operations grew. One of the reasons we turn to technology is that it can help speed things up, make them more efficient, and lessen the manual labor burden. Of course, that leads to economic savings through staff reduction, something that becomes increasingly important when the competition for market share grows. We're not entirely against that. Being able to compete is necessary for any business. In hospitality, however, guest experience will be determined more by what humans do than by what machines do.

Not long after computers became a common sight on every desktop in every hotel administration office, the welcome cards for VIP arrivals began to be printed off hundreds at a time. They all contained the same boring words.

"Welcome to our hotel. My team and I will do everything we can to make your stay comfortable. If there's anything I can do, please call Guest Services. Enjoy your stay."

Some hotels became "creative" and had two types of cards. One that said "welcome" and one that said "welcome back." Some hotels became what we would call "reverse creative" and used the General Manager's scanned signature on these "personal" welcome notes.

In a few cases, hoteliers probably realized how impersonal they had become. In those hotels, the card would also contain a handwritten note from a manager. Some of those were quite good and had personal touches like adding Kirsten's name to the welcome or providing a cell number saying, "If you have time, give me a call, and let's catch up over a coffee."

The impersonal, fully automated, machine-written, machine-signed welcome note has nothing to do with creating a warm, welcoming atmosphere, and it does nothing to make the guest feel recognized and personally welcomed.

Tullin's Café, Oslo: Playing your song was their tune for success

When Paul first started as a hotel security guard, SAS (Scandinavian Airlines), who owned the hotel he worked at, had just been awarded International Business Airline of the Year. They were "The Businessman's Airline" (apparently, the concept of businesswomen hadn't yet been invented), and the SAS hotels were "The Businessman's Hotel."

The introductory training was detailed and demanding, right down to the grooming booklet that stipulated men's hair had to be cut a centimetre or two above the collar and banned beards. (Paul has had a beard ever since the peach fuzz started growing on his chin, but nobody asked him to shave it off, so he pretended not to have read that page in the booklet.) Recognition and calling guests by name (Mr. This or Dr. That) was highly encouraged, although some staff members protested, saying in Norway, guests didn't want people to use their names. That might be viewed as good service when they were on holiday in Spain, but in Norway, it was "weird."

People are people though, so the servers and bell staff who followed the suggested procedures were the ones who received the largest tips, even at a time when tipping was also "weird" in Norway.

The hotel had 491 rooms, three restaurants, three bars, a nightclub, and conference facilities for up to about 1,000 people. With one exception, hotel staff were not allowed to visit restaurants or bars unless it was part of their job (i.e., managers or sales staff entertaining clients or prospects).

The one exception was a small restaurant that didn't have direct access from the hotel itself. The entrance was from the street, on a side of the building next to the entrance to the underground garage. Not only did staff have access to the restaurant and bar, but they were also given rebates on food and drink, and, with Norwegian alcohol prices in mind, that was a substantial pull.

During a boom period, the bean counters decided that giving rebates to staff, who visited the restaurant daily, was bad for the bottom line. They could fill the restaurant with full-price paying guests. Staff were still welcome but without the discount.

That same summer, a new bar/café opened across the street from the hotel, just as the office workers and most other people in Oslo departed on their summer holidays. The only people left in town were tourists and hotel staff. The tourists were often on all-inclusive package tours, where their meals were included and time to visit local cafés was limited. That could have been a disaster for the owner of the new café. Instead, it was the start of a booming business.

He came to the hotel and offered a discount to the staff. In the early days, two or three hotel staff members would drop in for a drink after work. The quiet, almost timid owner had recently relocated to the capital from a town further north in the country. His café had a very limited menu, so most people just had a couple of beers before going home for dinner or moving on to eat somewhere else.

The owner asked us what he could add to the menu that would make us happier. At some point, burgers and wings were added to the little list of peanuts and potato chips.

Soon enough, not only were more staff stopping by after work, many were eating and staying longer into the evening. Judging by their tired eyes at work the next day, some may have even stayed too long once or twice.

As the summer went by, the little café counted a growing number of hotel staff members amongst the clientele. It survived the summer. By September, the owner was on a first-name basis with many. He even learned their tastes in music, and when one of Paul's colleagues mentioned his favorite song, every time that colleague entered the café, the owner would put that song on the jukebox. (It almost drove Paul's colleague crazy, but there's no denying the recognition factor!)

When office workers started to return to the towers surrounding the hotel, the café became so packed it was impossible to get a table for happy hour on Fridays. To thank the hotel staff who had kept the beer flowing during the summer stillness, the owner of the café called the hotel security department every Friday at noon and asked, "How many?"

The hotel security staff had spent the morning checking in with colleagues in other departments, so anyone who wanted a drink at happy hour was sure to have a spot reserved. Their loyalty was rewarded, and the café continued to flourish.

We visited Oslo a few days before we left Europe for Canada. The café was still there. The restaurant at the hotel that was once the favorite haunt of staff had changed names and owners many times over the years. In hospitality, recognition and catering to guest needs is key to survival.

The River Inn, Washington, DC: Always a smile for us

The River Inn, located in the Foggy Bottom district of Washington, DC, is an all-suite, boutique hotel with 125 rooms. It's walking distance to both shopping in Georgetown and the State Department. In other words, it was the perfect location for our regular trips to the US capital, during which Paul attended the annual briefing of the Overseas Security Advisory Council (OSAC) at the State Department. Kirsten got her exercise walking through the streets of Georgetown, seeing the sights, and after a few years she had friends in the city to visit and have lunch with. Our annual trip the week before US Thanksgiving was a tradition that took place for more than a decade.

We found The River Inn the way many people find things these days. We did an internet map search and tried to find someplace affordable that was less than a 30-minute walk from the State Department. The easiest way to book in 2007 was to send an email inquiry. The reservations department answered promptly and, surprisingly, very personally. In the email, we had asked about local dining and shopping possibilities. Not only did they answer our question, but the booking agent also wrote what her favourite shops and restaurants were.

In the years that followed, although online booking improved immensely as the company that operated The River Inn, Modus Hotels, grew and centralized their booking office, we continued to book via email, and the booking agents continued to respond promptly and personally.

The doorman recognized us probably after our second visit and became our go-to guy for affordable airport transfers. He had an umbrella ready for us if it rained and a smile for us no matter the weather.

From year two, there was always a handwritten card and homemade cookies waiting in our room. Our most recent check-in at The River Inn was in November 2017. When the receptionist found our reservation in the system, he looked up at us and said, "Wow, you guys have been coming here for eleven years! That's awesome. Welcome back!" (He was probably only eleven years old the first time we checked in.) We had to count on our fingers to confirm that, indeed, we had been coming to the hotel for eleven years.

One year though, we didn't stay there. The River Inn was being renovated, so the reply to our email inquiring about a room said:

"Yes, of course, we are ready to welcome you here, but I would suggest you consider staying somewhere else. We will be undergoing noisy renovations in November. You would be more comfortable somewhere else. I can arrange for you to stay at one of our sister properties. It's only a few minutes' walk from here."

That year, we stayed at the Avenue Suites. It was newly renovated, in a great location, and suited us well. The next year, we were back at The River Inn.

Lots of very good hotels do a good job of making their guests feel welcome and recognized. But sometimes, the areas they slip up in are the areas they don't take responsibility for, such as the outsourced services on the property. In today's gig economy world, that can mean anything from concierge services to housekeeping and cleaning to bars, restaurants, or shopping outlets. Hotels like to say that these services are part of their offerings, but if something goes awry, they can be quick to explain why your problem isn't their responsibility.

The River Inn has a small restaurant and bar, Dish n' Drinks. It seats about 12–16 people at tables and about the same amount at the high tops in the bar area. It's not operated by the hotel, but the people who run it create the same warm atmosphere. Whether it's local people dropping in for a pre-event dinner before heading to the Kennedy Center or hotel guests coming in for a nightcap before retiring to their rooms, everyone is welcomed, and regulars are recognized.

We always made room for at least one dinner there during our annual week in Washington, and we made sure we were back in time for a quick drink in the bar almost every night. The bartender recognized us, entertained us with stories of his adventures in Alaska or college capers during his younger years, and grew to know what we liked to drink when we'd had a good day or bad. In recent years, we usually didn't even order. He'd say, "How was your day?" and then he'd say, "I've got just the thing." The "thing" was always just what we needed.

One of our favourite memories from The River Inn has more to do with fate than with personal recognition.

During our trip in 2017, the week was so packed with meetings that Paul's most important one was on Sunday before the workweek kicked off. From Monday to Friday, every day and every evening was packed with appointments.

Just before we departed Brussels on Friday, November 17, with a plan to stay until Saturday, November 25, Paul was informed that he needed to be back in the office for important meetings on November 21. We changed our flights, cancelled meetings, lunches, and dinners, and informed the hotel that we'd be checking out on Monday, November 20. Our disappointment only grew when, upon arriving back in Brussels at 7:00 a.m. after our overnight flight, the meetings Paul had been summoned back for were cancelled. Still, we're grateful when we look back on the twisted turns of events.

Since September, Paul had been reading a weekly blog called *Sunday Morning Joe*. The author was Joe Jacobi, the first American to win an Olympic gold medal in whitewater kayaking. Joe had connected with Paul on LinkedIn and they corresponded regularly. Joe was from DC but had moved to La Seu d'Urgell, in Catalunya, Spain, with his family. La Seu is where Joe won his gold medal.

As we cancelled all our plans and pondered what to do on the Monday before our evening flight back to Belgium, Paul noticed that Joe was posting pictures of a visit with his father near DC. We sent him a note saying it would be funny if we accidentally bumped into him as we wandered around Washington on a day when we suddenly had nothing to do. A few hours later, we met Joe in person for the first time. We invited him to join us for lunch at our hotel. Joe lives life as if it's a river. Upstream, downstream, rapids and calm water, Joe is a master of flow. What better place to meet a gold-medal-winning, kayak-paddling Olympian than The River Inn?

Kirsten often says things happen for a reason. It may or may not have been fate that intervened and gave us the opportunity to meet Joe, but the recognition we had received from the hotel and its restaurant over the years made it the obvious choice as the place for us to invite a stranger that quickly became a friend.

Skinny Duke's Glorious Emporium, Kelowna: Revisiting that '70s basement party

When your favourite restaurant names a pizza after you, that is an awesome example of personalized recognition. It's either that or a sign that you eat way too much pizza, but truth be told, we had only eaten pizza once at Skinny Duke's Glorious Emporium before COVID-19 temporarily closed their doors. Still, naming a pizza after us was likely one of the brightest, and most welcomed, signs of recognition we've ever experienced.

Paul's post-high school gap year lasted four decades. Travel for work and pleasure has taken him to over 60 countries. In the 20 years we've been together, we've had the great fortune of staying in some of the world's finest hotels, eating in multiple Michelin-star restaurants, and sitting in first class on world-renowned airlines. Some might think it strange that a relatively new restaurant designed to look like somebody's basement in 1977 that mainly serves pizza and a few fusion recipes could make our list of memorable places.

When it opened, Skinny Duke's Glorious Emporium brought with it the feel-good atmosphere from its big brother, BNA Brewing Co. We'd only been to BNA a couple of times, one of which was to see The Grapes of Wrath perform after being inducted into the Western Canada Music Hall of Fame. We can tell you about our connection to the band and why we were dancing like teenagers beside the city mayor as they belted out their hits from the '80s another time. Suffice to say, BNA has a vibe and a great local reputation.

The atmosphere wasn't all that Skinny Duke's brought with it from BNA when it opened. Some of BNA's staff took up the challenge of opening the new place too.

Paul grew up in Kelowna in the '60s and '70s. He saw quite a few basements during that time, including a fair number that transformed into party venues when someone's parents were out of town, or even when some were home but very understanding of the fact that their basement was full of teenagers, none of whom were nineteen (Canada's legal drinking age) and some of whom would consume alcohol.

Skinny Duke's hit the interior design nail on the head – right down to the old TVs playing the same shows and commercials Paul remembers and the same songs on the radio from his teenage years. It's almost like those four decades after high school never happened.

A lot of restaurants around the world have great interior design. Some are awesome. Some have views to die for. Some have celebrity chefs who create month-long queues for reservations just by adding their name to the restaurant. As we pointed out earlier though – and as we'll continue to do throughout this book – design, location, names, and fame are nothing if you don't have the right people in place.

One of the first things our first server did when we wandered in on a Saturday afternoon was ask us our names.

"I am trying to learn as many names as I can," she said, "and I'll try to remember yours next time you come."

We enjoyed ourselves that day and soon became regulars. That probably made it easy for her to remember our names, but soon enough, other servers knew our names without asking, as well as some of our favorite items on the menu and wine list.

Although the average age of the clientele rises dramatically when we walk in, we're treated like normal people. (Unlike another local restaurant where, after the server informed us their menus were online, a supervisor promptly stepped in, set down a paper menu and said, "We have these for people like you!" Paul's grey hair gave us away and told him we were likely not iPhone savvy enough to download their menu.)

At Skinny Duke's we're not "people like us," we're people. We're people they recognize, and we've become people who recognize them. Recognize and recommend, we should add.

In March 2020, when COVID-19 arrived in town and shut down restaurants and many other businesses, we said farewell to Skinny Duke's. The writing was on the wall and, despite almost no cases in our part of the province at the time, we decided Friday the Thirteenth would be a good day to have one last night out. The decision to spend it at "Skinny's" was an easy one.

In some parts of the world, being a server is a profession, not just a position. That's not too common in North America, where many young people do it as a summer job or while waiting for something better to come along. Finding people who care as much about their guests and doing their jobs properly is probably tricky, since so many view being a server as something very temporary, just done for the money.

Our server on that fateful Friday before lockdown hit the city knew her job was in jeopardy. Her attitude was different than many, though, and probably different from most people.

"I think I'll be losing my job in a few days," she said. "But if you think about it, this is a really interesting time to be alive. We're going to learn a lot!"

Skinny Duke's closed the next week. They were down but not out.

When restaurants were allowed to open for takeout and delivery, they were back on the scene.

To our enormous surprise, they honored us the first weekend by naming a pizza after us. Of course, we had to order "The Mox" right away, and we both went down to Skinny's when it was time to pick it up. That was the first time we met one of the owners. She was on hand to try to keep the ship afloat until the storm passed and businesses could again find calmer waters.

She knew we were the people the staff wanted to name a pizza after, and she wanted to thank us personally for being such good guests. What she showed us was that we had felt a warm welcome from day one because the owners had hired people like themselves. People who care – not only about their jobs and their paychecks, but about people and the world around us.

The surprise didn't just encourage us to try our namesake pizza pie though; it also led us to tell everyone we know about the unexpected experience. It brought back memories of the theme song from the sitcom *Cheers* that spoke about people's wish to go somewhere everyone knows their name.

In short, it made us feel special, included, and cared about. This was perhaps especially moving because it took place at a time when no one was struggling more than the hard-hit hospitality industry.

To us, our experiences at Tullin's Café, The River Inn, and Skinny Duke's show that when you recognize every guest as a person and not just a customer, you're laying great groundwork for success. Remember: It's personal, so be wary of trying to automate it!

What have you learned? What can you do?	
1	Everyone's an individual, and being recognized for who we are makes us feel good. If you can't remember a guest's name, acknowledge that you have met them and show that you appreciate them.
2	Guests feel when recognition is fake or driven by automation.
3	Remembering someone's personal preference reminds them of why they continue to choose you.
4	If you don't have time to personally recognize your VIPs, you have the wrong definition of a VIP.

- When have you been impressed by personal recognition? How can you use the experience to improve your own service?
- Think about which of our feel-good stories resonates most with you. What can you take from the story and add to your daily life?

Something Special: Freebies and Upgrades

Sometimes, when you're a regular at a restaurant or you travel enough to get "status" on an airline or hotel "loyalty" program, you're given a freebie. (We add the quotation marks because we don't believe many of those programs understand the concepts of loyalty or reward.)

Freebies can be as simple as the homemade cookies that accompanied the hand-written welcome note we always received at The River Inn. In hotels, you will often be given a card "good for one free breakfast" or a drink coupon that can be used in the bar. But when you go for breakfast, you will learn that your freebie is only good for one person (even if you registered two in your reservation), or only good for continental breakfast (even though you don't consider a roll with cheese, jam, and ham breakfast). When you get to the bar, you learn that the coupon is good for a glass of house red, house white, or domestic beer (even if you usually drink Stella Artois). Sometimes there is small print on the card that specifies the limitations of the free drink they are honouring your loyalty with. Sometimes there isn't.

If you want to do something special for a guest, do something special. Handing over a coupon raises expectations, but surprising the guest by limiting its value to a glass of warm white wine destroys them.

K*Rico, NYC: The best table in the house

During one of our visits to New York City, we were wandering around Greenwich Village on a sunny September evening. We stopped in for a drink at a bar and started the daily process of Googling nearby restaurants to find a place for dinner. It was difficult but fortunately not impossible to find a place that was within walking distance, affordable, and had more than a 2.5-star average review rating. The ones we found were fully booked until we clicked on Philip Marie. It had a good rating, it was nearby, and it had a table for two we could book.

Philip Marie is a small bistro, not unlike the ones you find in Europe. The food was good, and we enjoyed a bottle of house red alongside it. During our meal, a man we had seen sitting at a table across the room approached us. He was dressed casually and looked like your regular New Yorker.

"How's your meal?" he asked in a voice with a New Jersey accent, confirming he was a local. He also asked where we were from and why we were in New York. At some point, he mentioned that he owned the restaurant.

"Do you like steak?" he asked, which was a bit weird since we'd just had a nice dinner. However, we confirmed that we did, and he continued, "If you like steak, you should try my other restaurant."

He fumbled around in his pocket, looking for a business card and a pen. As he continued to talk about his Argentinian steakhouse, K*Rico, he scribbled something on the card.

"Here, if you come to my other restaurant, you'll get a free bottle of wine."

On the back of the K*Rico card, he had written "one free bottle of wine."

"Tomorrow is our last day in New York," we said.

"If you come tomorrow, I will be there!"

When we awoke the next morning, we googled K*Rico. It had great reviews. On opentable.com, it had been booked several hundred times that day. We decided we couldn't say no to a free bottle of wine, so we booked a table for 8:00 p.m.

We arrived at the restaurant and were guided to a table with crisp, white linen by a host who pulled Kirsten's chair out for her. This was by all first impressions an upmarket steakhouse. When he handed us the menu, the server asked what we'd like to drink. Paul fished out the card and said we had been given it by a man at Philip Marie the day before who had promised us a free bottle of wine.

The server opened the wine list and asked, "What would you like?" Bottles ranged in price from about $30 to several hundred. Not wanting to seem greedy, Paul picked something around the $50 mark.

There was a door near our table. A server or a host stood near the door, and servers went in through it with empty hands and returned carrying plates of delicious-looking food. When they passed, the awesome aromas of the chef's creations had our mouths watering.

Suddenly, from through that door, he appeared. The man we had met the day before. He was wearing an executive chef's uniform.

"Ah! You came!" he said. "I give out thousands of those cards a year and almost no one ever comes. Did you get your wine?"

We said we had just ordered it. Chef went over to the bar and talked to the sommelier. The sommelier showed him the bottle. Chef shook his head, said something, and then disappeared back through the door and down some steps to the kitchen.

The sommelier came to our table with a much more expensive wine than we had ordered and said, "Chef thought you might like this better."

Chef returned with the display tray of all the different cuts of steak on offer that the servers show customers. He explained all the cuts and then he looked at us and said, "Do you like ribeye?" We confirmed. "Do you like bourbon?" We confirmed.

He told us that he dry-aged all the steak in-house and that he had a bourbon-infused ribeye, that, if we promised we loved ribeye, he would prepare for us. It wasn't on the menu, and he told us what it would cost. He said it would be an awesome experience. We ordered it.

Having seen the size of the steaks, we ordered two sides to share and decided to skip starters and save room for dessert.

A server arrived and set two large starters down. Paul said there must be a mistake because we hadn't ordered starters. "No mistake," he said. "Chef thinks you should have these."

Chef arrived with a host, impeccably dressed in a double-breasted pinstripe suit. "This is my brother!" he said. "He runs front-of-house; I run back-of-house." The host explained we had the best table in the house. Some people may wonder how the best table in the house could be right beside the door to the kitchen, but he explained that he, Chef, another host, or a server would always be right outside the door. Since we were the closest table, we could always get quick service and attention if we needed anything.

When the steaks arrived, they were accompanied by four sides instead of two. Chef had decided we should have Brussels sprouts (we lived in Brussels at the time) and another typically European dish that was in season.

The steaks were melt-in-your-mouth good. Chef arrived about the time we swallowed our first bite. He was happy to hear that we liked them but told us to wait as he went off towards the bar.

He returned with two glasses of aged bourbon. "Take a small sip when you take the next bite of steak," he said. "You'll have an explosion of taste!" We did, and we did. So good in fact that we coined the term "awesomelicious" in an attempt to describe the experience.

Dessert, coffee, and a picture with Chef rounded off our evening. When we paid the bill, we paid for what we ordered. The free bottle of wine was free, and it was more expensive than the one we had politely tried to order. The starters were free. The extra sides were free. The bourbon we were given to taste alongside the steak was free.

"Exceeding expectations" is a hospitality cliché, but the way we were treated at K*Rico was so far beyond our expectations, we would be understating things if we used that cliché here.

Needless to say, if we ever hear of anyone who is going to New York City, we always tell them to try K*Rico. We've been back a couple of times ourselves too, and we know a few friends who now visit every time they are in the Big Apple themselves. The "free bottle of wine" has likely paid for itself many times over.

We can't recall ever recommending a place that offered us a free drink and then limited our choice to the cheapest glass of wine on offer.

Fairmont Hotel Vancouver: Upgrade or upsell

Although Paul worked in security for his entire career, there was a time when the company was still small and security – it pains us to write these next few oxymoronic words – "wasn't important enough" to be a full-time corporate position. We use quotation marks because those aren't our words; they were the words of Paul's superiors at the time.

Alongside his responsibilities for corporate safety and security, managing the newly started loyalty programs, travel agent commission payments, and even database marketing (the pre-cursor to digital marketing) all fell under Paul's responsibilities. It was an awesome learning experience, even if it did have him working 13–15 hours a day.

When loyalty programs first started, airlines (and slightly later, hotels) used them to reward their loyal travellers and fill empty seats (or rooms) at no cost. They weren't even meant to be profit centres. In the hotel company, hotels paid the loyalty program for each guest night that earned loyalty program points for the program member. When a guest stayed free on a reward night, the loyalty program paid the hotel a fixed rate. At corporate level, the cost hotels paid for guests accruing points was meant to match the revenue the loyalty program paid hotels for guests who used points for free stays. Since people accrued more in some places (think: places only businesspeople travel) and wanted to stay for free more in others (think: London, Paris, or a romantic resort), complicated calculations were necessary to balance everything out between the different hotels and the program.

Somewhere along the line, somebody decided that loyalty programs could and should become profitable. Governments decided that points people earned should be taxed like income, and everything seemed to change. In Europe, where governments love taxes, you can often buy a flight cheaper than you can fly for "free" using your points.

In the "old days," say the early 1990s, if you were a gold card member, you could often get upgraded to business class or a suite in a hotel. Today, you can get an upgrade against a deduction of a certain (usually astronomical) number of points.

Sometimes, when hotels are heavily booked, we've experienced being "upgraded" to an executive floor with the explanation that the "upgrade" doesn't include the privilege of visiting the executive floor lounge or other amenities included with stays on the executive floor. Riding the elevator a few more floors is not an "upgrade."

There are good exceptions, though. During a security conference in Vancouver a few years ago, we were given a true upgrade at the Fairmont Hotel Vancouver. It didn't happen by chance, but a friend knew the manager and whispered in his ear that we would be staying there.

The hotel was special to Paul. When he was 13, he accompanied his father on a business trip to Vancouver. It wasn't really about business; it was more of a father-son bonding trip that included a stay at the Hotel Devonshire and the first professional hockey game Paul ever saw. (Vancouver beat Atlanta 5–0, so it was a memorable event for him.)

The Hotel Devonshire was kitty-corner to the Hotel Vancouver. Today, the Hotel Devonshire has been replaced by a glitter-and-glass building housing HSBC Bank. The Hotel Devonshire was a nice, small hotel, but it wasn't the Hotel Vancouver. Without knowing, or even dreaming, that he would ever work in hotels, not to mention hotels as prestigious and famed as the Hotel Vancouver, Paul remembers looking out his hotel room window, wondering who all the fancy people were that entered and exited the five-star place across the street. Movie stars? Media moguls? Hockey players?

Fast forward too many years to count and it was our turn to find out. Just like the day when he almost didn't apply for the job that started his career, Paul still gets butterflies in his stomach every time he enters a fancy or famous hotel. Checking in at the Hotel Vancouver was one of those occasions. Checking in and learning that we had been upgraded to their executive floors, with all the privileges included, almost caused him to throw himself down and cry, "I'm not worthy!" Wayne's World style – but fortunately he kept his composure, and we thanked the receptionist and headed to the elevators.

The room was wonderful. The lounge served happy hour drinks and a great breakfast, but the biggest surprise was the soaps, shampoos, and other amenities. They were all personalized for Paul. Had this not been included in our upgrade, we'd never have known they did it at all, but at the Hotel Vancouver, they didn't do upgrades halfway.

We've booked the Hotel Vancouver and other Fairmont properties more times in the few years since our upgrade than we ever booked in all previous years. We don't usually stay on the club floors, but we often stay in their hotels.

Upgrades are like freebies. They should be something that is offered to someone who, due to loyalty or circumstance, deserves them. If you dilute them, deduct points, or charge anything for them, that's an upsell – not an upgrade – and upselling is a tricky form of marketing.

British Airways: Downgrade with an upside

In 1994, Paul was on holiday in Beijing, China. He was travelling on standby tickets and getting a return flight was proving difficult. SAS was overbooked. Swissair at first said yes, but upon noticing Paul was a hotel employee at SAS and not an airline employee, decided not to honour his staff ticket. Finally, after a long wait in the Beijing Airport (which wasn't as comfortable then as you would find today), British Airways accepted Paul and his colleague onto the flight to Heathrow, where they would have plenty of time to transfer to an SAS flight back to Oslo. The standby tickets they had were for business class, but British Airways said they were fully booked in business and offered only economy. Paul had to be at work the day after returning, so getting back was more important than what seat he was given.

It would turn out to be an adventurous journey. While the flight was airborne, the IRA had attacked Heathrow Airport. Utter chaos awaited on the ground, with delays before the flight could land and delays before a gate was available. Thousands of people were stuck and stranded in the terminal. The flights to Oslo had long since been due to depart, but they were encouraged to try to check in anyway since nothing was clear about anything. The last two seats on a flight that should have departed an hour earlier were available, and they boarded just as the flight was ready for pushback. Pushback didn't happen, though, as the airport and flight paths had been closed again. The captain on the SAS plane gave updates every 15 minutes, helping to keep everyone on board calm. At one point he suggested that he had asked the tower for permission to taxi around "to make it more difficult for the IRA by giving them a moving target," although it's unclear how many passengers shared his sense of humour. Long story short, Paul made it home. But what about that downgrade on the flight from Beijing?

Once Paul and his colleague were seated on board, a purser came over and thanked them for accepting the downgrade. They were the ones who needed to be thankful since their tickets weren't technically valid for British Airways, and they were only standby anyway. The purser continued by saying that he hoped they could be understanding during meal service. They had been accepted on the flight so late that catering couldn't be adjusted. The purser promised them food but said that they would bypass them initially so they could give as many paying passengers as possible their preferred menu choices. This was all done very discreetly, and it's unlikely any nearby passengers even noticed as most were busy finding their seats and cramming carry-on bags into the overhead bins.

When the flight was airborne and meal service started, it wasn't the purser, but two flight attendants who were responsible for Paul's seat. As they rolled the meal trolley down the aisle, they casually skipped Paul's side when they passed his row. The purser was right behind them though, and with a wink and a whispered thanks, he placed two mini-bottles of champagne on their tray tables.

The flight attendants returned later and apologized for "missing them" on the first pass. Dinner was served.

That flight was memorable because of the many small gestures the BA staff made to make it happen. The station manager accepted their non-revenue tickets even though SAS didn't have an agreement with BA for that type of ticket. The purser told Paul upfront upon boarding about the lack of catering and explained the approach they would take. He also informed his flight attendant colleagues. To Paul, his colleague, and all the other passengers on board, everything went as it normally does on a long-haul flight. The BA team was excellent at communicating, collaborating, and contributing to making that happen.

What have you learned? What can you do?	
1	A freebie is a gift, not a cheap marketing ploy. They pay off in the long term, not the short.
2	Restricting the value of a freebie can feel like unwrapping a lump of coal at Christmas.
3	Upgrades don't drive short-term revenue, but they can create long-term loyalty.
4	Moving someone to a business class suite or offering a better bottle of wine is not an upgrade if you take money or deduct points for it.
5	If you provide an upgrade, it should include all the amenities of the upgraded product.
6	If you need to downgrade someone, empathize with them. Also, a little extra service reduces the risk of complaints and compensation.
➤ Try to remember an upgrade, downgrade, or freebie that left you feeling appreciated, and then try to remember one that left you feeling "meh." What differentiated them?	

Navigating Cultural Differences

Bjørn and Paul met the day they both joined the staff at SAS Scandinavia Hotel (now a Radisson Blu) in Oslo, Norway, just before the summer of 1987. Bjørn was a bellboy, and Paul was a security guard. They were very different personalities but became best friends. Bjørn was Paul's best man at our wedding.

Bjørn rose quickly through the ranks at the hotel. Bellboy to doorman, front desk clerk to night manager. Service was the most natural thing in the world to him, and no guest need went unaddressed. One night when the hotel and the city were completely overbooked, with no available rooms within 100 miles, Bjørn gave the keys to his apartment to a guest who arrived after midnight and after the last room had been filled.

He went on to hotel school, and upon graduation he was given a management traineeship in Beijing, China. Several months after he'd arrived in Beijing, the hotel security manager came to Oslo on a week-long visit to shadow Paul and learn more about the corporate culture of the company.

One of the security officers at Paul's hotel was married to a woman who spoke and wrote Chinese, and she furnished Paul with a sign he could take to the airport so the arriving colleague would recognize his name. The security manager from Beijing understood very little English and spoke even less. On the drive into town, Paul mentioned that his friend, Bjørn, worked at the hotel in Beijing. When he said that, Paul thought he saw a little flicker of recognition flash in his colleague's eyes.

An official interpreter from the Chinese Embassy arrived the next day to ensure the security manager from Beijing could properly understand everything. Before the day's work started, the two men spent about 15 minutes getting to know one another over a coffee. Afterwards, the interpreter approached Paul and said that the security manager thought he might have understood something Paul had said on the drive from the airport.

"He said you know someone at his hotel," the interpreter said.

"Yes," Paul replied. "My best friend, Bjørn, recently started as a management trainee there."

The interpreter translated for the security manager, whose eyes immediately lit up, and he smiled from ear to ear.

The two men chatted back and forth excitedly for a few moments before the interpreter translated for Paul.

"That wonderful man can become whatever he wants to become in China! He is the first white person your company has sent to Beijing who understands that the Chinese are people."

Bjørn did go on to have an amazing career in China in a business completely unrelated to hotels. Doors were opened by his service mentality and he grasped the opportunities they provided.

Not everything translates directly and easily from culture to culture, but a surprising amount of what makes us human can be applied around the world, especially in the hospitality business. As social media and globalization bring us all closer together, what at first glance may appear to be huge differences fade away once we become better acquainted with our fellow humans.

To grow his cultural awareness and gain an understanding of what was on the minds of people he met during his travels, Paul always read local papers and used stories from them in his workshops to make them as relevant as possible to the audience.

When papers he could read and understand were harder to come by, he would try to watch in-flight movies that were subtitled in English. This was always helpful when he flew to China. On one trip, the movie he watched was about a girl who worked in an office. She was popular, in part because her boyfriend was a rock star. At the start of the movie, her boyfriend breaks up with her because he has an audition on the Chinese version of *Idol* or *X-Factor*, and his agent thinks he'll have a better story and a better chance of winning if he's single. Paul was left wondering what had become of the cultural differences everyone said were so hard to overcome.

Paul has often said that if you took someone off the streets of Vancouver, Canada, and dropped them in the streets of Johannesburg, South Africa, they would become very careful and hesitant in their behaviour. Everything would look and sound different. Cars would be coming from the opposite direction compared to what they were used to. They may have heard about high crime statistics or protests and poverty, and thus their behaviour would be quite protective in nature.

What we sometimes forget is that the opposite is also true. If a South African person was dropped off in the middle of Vancouver, everything would look and sound different to them. Cars would be driving on the "wrong" side of the street, and while shopping, they might feel cheated when provincial, government, and harmonized sales tax were only added once they reached the cashier.

Being aware of biases is a great first step towards overcoming or reducing the impact they have on us. It reminds us that stripping away the thin layers of language, religion, culture, and tradition reveals fundamental similarities between people. Most people are proud of who they are and where they're from. When they travel, they carry their pride along, but they also have the baggage of uncertainty about the unknown culture they are visiting. This combination can mask itself in a quiet, reserved way, but it can also be projected as arrogant-sounding demands that far exceed those they would normally make in the comfort of their own community.

The motto of the Hard Rock Café is "Love All, Serve All." It's probably harder than it sounds, but by reminding yourself that people are people, you can help move beyond the uncertainty and fear that is often felt on both sides of the front desk when the first travellers from a new country or new culture arrive.

Le Trappiste, Brussels: The brasserie that closes when tourists arrive

Serge wasn't the only Belgian server who had perfected "Spin the Bottle Service." He was one of the first we noticed, and he was one of the people who noticed us. In the mind of a guest, recognition is even more important than spinning the bottle. Everyone is an individual, and most people appreciate being viewed as a person more than just as a customer, tourist, or worse, a representative of a target market segment.

When Paul arrived in Europe, two experiences especially drove home the difference when it was holiday or vacation time. In Norway in the late 1970s, everything closed for five days at Easter. Without being forewarned, Paul almost starved during his first Easter in Trondheim. Fortunately, there was a café at the train station that stayed open, so although he may have lost a few pounds, he was able to get coffee and a bun with cheese.

As summer rolled around, people started talking about "industriferien," which, simply translated, is the "industrial holiday." It wasn't quite as universal as Easter, but a huge number of businesses shut down for three to four weeks in July. Similarly, in France and Belgium (probably due to some European agreement from the Middle Ages, or at least the onset of the industrial age), businesses shut down in August.

A lot of this has changed, of course. Norway now has 7-Eleven and a multitude of other places that will feed and caffeinate you no matter what day of the year it is, and many factories all over Europe, including France and Belgium, have robots that don't take holidays, so production never ceases. Some places like to stick to tradition, though.

Le Trappiste is a small brasserie in Brussels. It is located on Avenue de la Toison d'Or, a street it shares with high-end shops like Tiffany, Chanel, and Louis Vuitton. We had lived in Brussels for a few years before we ventured in. From the outside, it was a nondescript kind of place, flanked on one side by a dime-a-dozen restaurant franchise and on the other by a fast-food fried chicken chain. During summer there is an outdoor terrace, and if we walked by on our way to the nearby cinema, the people on the patio at Le Trappiste all appeared to be beer-drinking Belgians of upper-middle age. Except for the lady with the blue hair, bright pink eye shadow, and layer upon layer of rouge and black mascara. She was there each time we passed, drinking something that looked like a gin and tonic.

We're not sure when or why we first set foot in the door at Le Trappiste. We do know that we went back many, many times during our decade in Brussels, and we've made it a point to try to have lunch or a drink there whenever we've passed through since.

When Paul was a kid, his grandmother found him very easy to feed when she cared for him and his two brothers while his parents enjoyed a European holiday in 1966. When she asked what he would like to eat, his answer was always macaroni and cheese, no matter if it was breakfast, lunch, or dinner time. If he couldn't have that, he would settle for a grilled cheese sandwich.

His palate hasn't changed, so the first time he was in Paris, he sat at a café and ordered a croque monsieur, which was the closest the menu came to grilled cheese. It changed his world. He now prefers croque monsieurs to grilled cheese, but alas, they're harder to come by these days. Even in France and Belgium, ordering a croque can easily net you a regular old grilled cheese sandwich.

Not at Le Trappiste. We ordered two croque monsieurs, a Rochefort 10 (11.2% abv) beer for Paul and a Rochefort 8 ("only" 9% abv) for Kirsten. The beers were delivered at the perfect temperature along with "Trappiste Rochefort" glasses, and, of course, they were served with "Spin the Bottle Service." The croque monsieurs were not grilled cheese sandwiches. They were the real deal, and it was quickly clear that Le Trappiste would be a restaurant we returned to.

Soon enough, we were regulars. The servers in their black trousers, white shirts, and long white aprons recognized us. Our favourite, Rudi, started bringing us our Rocheforts before we even ordered them, and he expressed surprise if ever we ordered anything other than a croque for lunch.

When you become a regular at a place that cares about how they operate, the people who work there care about you. On Kirsten's birthday one year, Paul was travelling and wouldn't return home until evening. She went to Le Trappiste to treat herself to a birthday drink.

"Ou est monsieur?" Rudi asked when she entered on her own. When she said Paul was travelling and she wanted to treat herself to a birthday drink, Rudi promptly returned with a slice of cheesecake, adorned with a candle, and a glass of champagne – on the house, of course.

Tourists who only visit Brussels during tourist season will never know what they're missing. Some tourists who visit Le Trappiste don't even know what they're getting. They complain about slow service, arrogant servers, and worn steps down to the toilets. Le Trappiste is not McDonald's, so service isn't meant to be super speedy, and we'll cover perceptions of arrogance in the next section about Les Garnements, Paris. And the steps? Step number nine is about a millimetre higher than the other fifteen or so steps, and guests – unless they are regulars – sometimes trip on their first few visits to the facilities. Even though Le Trappiste closes during "peak season" and lies in a tourist zone, it is always packed with familiar faces speaking local dialects of French.

"Location, location, location" is a cliché often used in real estate, hotel, and restaurant businesses as the three keys to success. Le Trappiste is, no doubt, in a good location, but their success is service. Not just "Spin the Bottle Service," which of course they do. It's also about giving their customers what they want – good, traditional, affordable food and drink. It's about recognizing the regulars and caring for and about them professionally. Even with technology that can tell us a guest is a regular, real recognition is about people, and staff turnover at Le Trappiste during the many years we visited was almost zero.

That's why they always recognized us, even when we returned a year after we'd moved to Canada.

Les Garnements, Paris: Don't ask if they'll be busy

Some people, even people from France (or perhaps mostly people from France), say that God created Paris to have someplace to put all the arrogant people. We think it was Stephen Clarke, an English author living in Paris, who taught us that in one of his books. In any case, for some reason, some people (perhaps most people not living in France) perceive all French people to be arrogant and Parisian people especially so. Our perception is different. We think it is all just a big misunderstanding and, perhaps, mainly a misunderstanding of Parisian/French humour.

In 2015, Paul and his counterparts from seven of the world's largest hotel companies were honoured by the Overseas Security Advisory Council (OSAC) at the US State Department. In a lavish ceremony at the Ritz Carlton in Georgetown, Washington, DC, the members of the Hotel Security Working Group (HSWG) were each given an achievement award for their contributions. Unfortunately, the group's French member from Accor Hotels was unable to attend.

Paul and a UK-based HSWG colleague took it upon themselves to hand deliver the crystal globe to their Paris-based friend. It was up to him to decide on a suitable venue for the small ceremony and dinner. Like all security leaders in the hotel world, even the ones from the world's largest hotel groups, budgets were limited, so needless to say the ceremony was not held at a Ritz Carlton or anything ritzy in Paris.

They met on a January evening at 7:00 p.m. at a Holiday Inn near Gare de Lyon, where one of the three was staying. The hotel is easily found from Gare de Lyon, especially after dark, because there is a three-story-high neon sign proclaiming "SEX SHOP" in bright yellow on the end of the building that faces the station.

Dinner reservations had been made for 8:30, so there was time for a drink beforehand. The streets between Gare de Lyon and the Bastille twist and turn, and long story short, the group got lost. When they finally found a bar, it was a simple student bar that only sold beer. That was okay, but time had been ticking, so the group ordered three half-pints of lager, which was the only beer available. Three full pints were placed in front of them.

"Sorry, we only ordered half pints," said the French-speaking member of the group.

"Yes, and you only paid for half pints, but we only have full pint glasses, so we just filled them up."

Not wanting to waste the precious liquid, they emptied the pints, and the group set off to find their restaurant. Before too long they were lost again, so some Googling was necessary before they finally arrived outside Les Garnements. The restaurant had been chosen by someone at Accor who knew our budget and the best brasseries in Paris that would fit it. Les Garnements was a small brasserie, quite nondescript, with simple wooden tables and chairs, a small bar counter near the entrance, and old newspapers covering the walls. It was also packed.

"We're here!" exclaimed our friendly Frenchman to the host. "We have a reservation."

"You had a reservation and you weren't here," was the answer. It was true. He added, "We're full."

Paul doesn't speak or understand much French, so after a couple of minutes of incomprehensible chit-chat, which seemed friendly enough, the restaurant host said, "Follow me."

A small table, behind a half wall that separated the restaurant from the kitchen and the steps down to the toilets, had been cleared and set for three people. The food was impeccable, the wine was wonderful, and the price even fit the meager budget. Around 11:00 p.m., the host/barman/server asked if it was okay if he locked the door.

"No problem," said the UK representative in the group. "It's getting late anyway; we should be going."

"Non, mon ami," said the representative from France. "He only means to officially close, and then everyone will start smoking."

The door was locked, the blinds were lowered, and right on cue, about 37 diners started spewing smoke from their Gauloises and Gitanes. The loophole in French anti-smoking laws was being exploited.

When he asked about locking the door, the host had also noticed the small trophy on the table. Once the doors were locked and blinds were shut, he was back with three small glasses and a bottle of cognac. He poured a glass for each of the party so they could properly celebrate whoever was being awarded for whatever they were being awarded for.

We visited Les Garnements several times between 2016 and 2018, when we left for Canada. On one particularly rainy afternoon, we sought refuge there. By then, we knew Laurent and Xavier by name.

We ordered a glass of wine and told Xavier we were just there to escape the rain. Paul then asked, "Are you busy tonight? We'd like to come for dinner."

"It's only 3 o'clock! How would I know if we're busy tonight?" Xavier shrugged and walked away. Some tourists might think of this as typical Parisian arrogance. It's not. Xavier was back a few moments later, refilled our glasses and said, "Come for dinner. Then you will find out if we're busy tonight!"

When we arrived for dinner, the same table he always gave us was set, but not in the usual way. In addition to the typical red-and-white checkered paper placemat, knife, fork, and wine glass for each person, there were also two champagne flutes. Xavier knew that although we didn't speak French, we had become European enough to enjoy a "coupe" before dinner.

Visiting Les Garnements in Paris became like visiting friends for us. They knew us. They accepted us, even when we had an extra enjoyable evening with two of our Parisian friends and entertained the restaurant with a round of "Alouette, Gentille Alouette" that the waitress and Xavier joined in on. One of our Parisian friends even proclaimed that we were at a good restaurant before he looked at the menu. He could tell just by the aromas that floated out from the kitchen.

There are thousands of brasseries in Paris and hundreds of top 10, top 20, and best brasseries of Paris lists. We're not sure Les Garnements is on any of them. To us though, they're masters of recognizing return guests. The first time we visited after Paul had gone with his hotel security colleagues, Xavier remembered that he had seen Paul before.

On what we thought would be our last visit to Paris before moving to Canada, we had Sunday lunch at Les Garnements.

The wine glasses were engraved with the logo and name of the restaurant. We asked Xavier if we could buy six glasses to take with us as a memory of all the good times we'd had there.

"Normally, yes," he said, "but yesterday was a busy Saturday, so we broke a few. I don't have any to sell."

We asked if he would order some for us if we promised to come back one more time before our move.

Today, with every glass of wine we drink at home, we remember Les Garnements. We remember Laurent and Xavier, who recognized us after our first visits, and we are also reminded that the myth about arrogant Parisians is just that: a myth.

Learning to bypass bias: From Kuwait to Shanghai

One of the easily overlooked obstacles we face in our daily lives is bias. We are often experts at assumption, forming opinions as fast as our eyes and ears send impulses to our brains. There are big benefits to recognizing that these opinions are bias and that a little more looking, listening, and thinking can help provide more realistic information of who someone is and how we can best communicate with and serve them.

In the early 1990s, a hotel in Kuwait was taken over by the invading Iraqi army. Fortunately, no one at the hotel was killed or physically injured. When the army retreated, the hotel was set on fire and seriously damaged. The rebuilding process took a couple of years. Paul visited the hotel prior to its reopening. At first glance, Kuwait was like many of its Middle Eastern neighbours at the time: a small country with a growing and increasingly modern capital city. Most locals wore traditional Arabic dress, and restaurants and coffee shops were segregated with sections for women and families apart from sections where men were allowed.

The local security manager was also responsible for human resources in the hotel. He had a true passion for hospitality, education, and training. He wanted Paul to experience as much as possible during the few days Paul was there; he especially wanted to visit as many hotels, restaurants, and coffee shops as possible so Paul could gain an understanding of how things worked in the country, what the competitor hotels had, and how his own hotel could reopen and become the best hotel in the country.

As they drove from place to place and afternoon was starting to become evening, Paul noticed that his local colleague looked at his watch almost incessantly. They had recently taken a break for prayer time, so Paul thought that the man felt an obligation to get home to his family. He had told Paul that he was married with two almost-grown sons. Paul had visions of a quiet, conservative family in his head, and he told his colleague that it was okay to drop him at the hotel so he could enjoy the evening with his family.

"No, it's okay, let's visit another coffee shop!" Paul's colleague replied, and off they went to another mall, another hotel, and another hole-in-the-wall coffee shop.

Finally, just before 8:00 p.m., Paul's colleague said, "If it's okay with you, I'll drop you back at the hotel now."

"Of course!" said Paul. "You should be home with your family."

"No, it's not that! I'm so happy you're here. You're my excuse! You see, my wife has become obsessed with jogging, and if I am home before eight, she'll insist that I go jogging too! I just want to spend my evenings with my feet up watching TV!"

Boom! Paul's bias was blown away.

We can have many experiences like that, but being biased has a sneaky way of coming back and biting us from time to time.

Although its original meaning was to trick sailors into joining a ship's crew, the term "shanghaied" has come to mean being tricked into going somewhere against one's will. Another English term for it might be "taken for a ride" by an unscrupulous taxi driver, something that Paul often experienced during our years in Copenhagen. When taxi drivers heard his less-than-perfect Danish accent, they would often suggest a longer route home from the airport when he returned from business trips. This is something that, unfortunately, was attempted by other taxi drivers in other cities during our many travels over the years.

Interestingly, one place Paul wasn't shanghaied by a taxi driver was in Shanghai itself. It was Christmas 1996 and Paul was visiting his friend Bjørn in Beijing. It was, in too many ways to mention, a very memorable Christmas. We'll spare those stories for another time. Between Christmas and New Year's, Paul visited Shanghai. In those days, before high-speed rail lines had been built between the cities, the quickest way to travel was by air, and flying first class was – for an international traveller – only slightly more expensive than coach. Paul splurged.

When the flight was called, Paul left the comfort of the first-class lounge and joined the throng of people lined up at the gate. While he was standing in line, a local gentleman approached him and said, "Didn't I see you in the lounge? No need to stand here!" He led Paul past the queue, and they were allowed to board first. As they entered the aircraft, a flight attendant handed them each a nicely wrapped gift. Paul's turned out to be a fine leather belt with an Air China buckle. He wore it for years.

Upon arrival in Shanghai, the sun was out and it wasn't too cold. That was fortunate because the queue for taxis to the city was extremely long. It took forty-five minutes before Paul was at the front of the queue. A white-gloved attendant opened the door and Paul jumped in.

"The Sofitel Hotel on Nanking Road, please," Paul said.

The driver gave him a blank stare. Paul repeated the destination very slowly. The stare remained in place. The queue attendant shouted at the driver. The driver shouted back. The attendant informed Paul that the driver didn't speak English.

"I'm going to the Sofitel on Nanking Road," Paul told him.

"Hotels and streets have different names in Chinese," the attendant said. "You're holding up the line. Go now or go to the back of the line."

Paul motioned to the driver and off they went. Soon enough they were speeding along on a wide, new freeway. Paul was comfortable and thought perhaps the driver had understood. After all, Sofitel was an internationally renowned brand and Nanking Road, whatever it was called in Chinese, was one of its most famous streets. At least it was to Paul.

Suddenly they weren't on the freeway anymore. They were driving down winding narrow streets lined by buildings that looked old and poorly maintained. A few minutes later, they were up on a freeway again. Then they were back on narrow roads with more potholes than pavement. This continued long enough for Paul to accept the fact that he was being shanghaied in Shanghai. He just wondered for how long and how much.

The taxi screeched to a halt. The driver switched the meter off and said something to Paul. Paul looked around and saw a building across the street. The word "Hotel" was on the wall beside the entrance, but it certainly wasn't the Sofitel. The driver jumped out and ran over to a policeman directing traffic at a nearby intersection. They talked, the policeman shrugged, and the taxi driver disappeared into the hotel. Moments later, he exited with a beaming smile and sprinted back across the street to the cab. He chatted away, flipped on the meter, and they were off again. Not long after, the cab swung up the winding drive that led to the main entrance of the brand new, five-star Sofitel.

Upon checking in, Paul received a card from the hotel as he'd done in many hotels and restaurants in Beijing. It listed the hotel address in Chinese and some of the most common city sights in both English and Chinese as well. All you had to do was hand the card to a doorman or taxi driver, and they would take you to your desired destination. Paul kicked himself for not having the hotel in Beijing write the name of the Shanghai Sofitel for him before he'd left. It would, he thought, have saved him a lot of time and likely some money if he'd had it when he jumped in the taxi at the Shanghai airport.

He was wrong. In his room, there was an information folder with the most common destinations in Shanghai, how long you should expect a taxi to take, and what you could expect it to cost. Paul had paid less for his ride than the amount listed in the folder.

His bias had beaten him again. While he was certain he was being Shanghaied, his driver was giving him the equivalent of "Spin the Bottle Service" by taking a shorter, less expensive route to his destination.

It's hard to avoid our bias, but remember that underneath the layers of language, looks, and culture, and behind our own preconceptions and expectations, we're all human. Some will shanghai you, some won't, and at the end of the day, a lot of us just want to put our feet up and watch TV.

What have you learned? What can you do?	
1	Despite visible differences – no matter culture, religion, gender, race, ability, or age – people are more similar than first impressions may give.
2	Awareness of personal bias is key in communicating with and understanding others.
3	Empathy can help reduce the impact of personal bias on your decision making.

- Take some time to reflect on experiences when your first impression was wrong. How did your personal bias get in the way? What happened to change your first impression?
- What "hidden resources" do you have on your team? Languages? Cultural backgrounds? What can you learn from them? How can your team benefit from them?

Fancy Doesn't Have to Mean Cold and Formal

Over the years, we've been privileged to travel first class, stay in five-star hotels, and eat in Michelin-star restaurants. When given the choice though (and even when cost isn't our biggest consideration) we'll often choose more down-to-earth options.

First-class, five-star, or Michelin-star service is always close to perfect, but it often feels far from personal. There are great exceptions to the rule, and in this section, we'll look at how a mother and son team introduced family friendliness to one of Brussels' high-end sports and wellness clubs. We'll also share a story of a Michelin-star restaurant that gives you a warm and comfortable atmosphere in which to enjoy their top-flight cuisine.

Top Délice: A treat at the retreat for Brussels' elite

It can't be easy being from Brussels. The capital of Belgium is the capital of the European Union, but often wins "awards" as the most boring place for tourists in Europe. If you draw a triangle between the famous cities of Paris, London, and Amsterdam, Brussels is a dot somewhere in the middle.

Most people from Brussels speak French, but the city is surrounded by Flemish language suburbs. Grand Place, located in the city center, is a UNESCO world heritage site. Surrounded by opulent guildhalls, the city's Town Hall, and the city museum (which is in a building the French call the King's House, or *Maison du Roi*, and the Flemish call the Bread House, or *Broodhuis*), it is considered one of the finest squares in Europe.

Like many capital cities, Brussels is teeming with lobbyists. Throw in the fact that it is where NATO headquarters is located and that it's the capital of 27 countries in addition to its own, and you have a major melting pot of international politicians and playmakers, many of whom have fairly substantial expense accounts.

When it's time to relax, work out, or mingle with other people who can charge large sums of money to their corporate accounts or foreign government ministries, one of the places to go is Aspria Royal La Rasante. One of Brussels' oldest, upper-class tennis and grass hockey clubs, Royal La Rasante has a fair share of Brussels' own elite in their member archives. In addition to the many tennis courts, multiple swimming pools, salon, spa, and fitness areas, the club also boasts a hotel or club residence with 16 rooms and three suites.

Of course, if you have all the amenities listed above, you also need to cater to the food and drink needs of members and their guests.

Thanks to a deal between the company Paul worked for and Aspria, despite the lack of an expense account, we enjoyed membership at the club for the last five or six years of our time in Brussels. Kirsten worked in the spa for the final few years, and since it was on the way home from Paul's office, we spent a great deal of time using the fitness facilities. After a good workout, it was also nice to restore some balance to the body by enjoying a beer, a glass of wine, or a meal.

During the first year of our membership, the restaurant, bar, and outdoor terrace were not too busy. The meals we had there were not close to the standard one would expect either. When the English wellness company Aspria acquired La Rasante, the food and drink offering was outsourced to a mother-and-son team, and the restaurant was rebranded Top Délice.

Maria was a Greek woman who had run restaurants in Brussels for a good few years, and Alex was her son. Together they were the brains behind a transformation that didn't alter the look of the space but changed the feel of the entire club while we were there. By the time we left, Top Délice was full almost every night of the week – and good luck getting a table on the patio if by chance the sun shone in Brussels.

Maria's other son, Theo, was also an employee; in fact, almost all of the service staff Maria brought in seemed to be local Belgian kids, and a large percentage of them had Greek heritage, so it was as common to hear them yelling orders to each other in Greek as French. The menu was typical for any Belgian brasserie, with the odd specialty from the Eastern Mediterranean thrown in with a few international favourites.

They were catering to a diverse and demanding crowd. Many of the members had grown up on the sunny side of life, no matter if they were local or from another European country, from Russia, or from further afield. In such a varied crowd, where everyone brings their own expectations, it can't be easy to appease everyone's taste. Add in the challenge of having to meet the requirements of the club owners, including that it is a member- and guest-only space, and you can start to see that there is no simple recipe for success.

From our perspective, Top Délice hit the most important nail in hospitality squarely on the head: knowing that people are people. Yes, some people have great expectations about how they should be served, how much more important they are than a simple server, or how different (better) their culture is than the local culture they just happen to be gracing with their presence, but scrape away the thin layer of culture, background, and what people are used to, and you'll find that people are people. Children are the best example because, at their young age, they haven't learned the differences between culture, class, gender, and race that somehow get in the way later in life.

Top Délice treated people like people. Alex knew every little kid in the club and always had a smile, joke, or game for them. Maria would float through the restaurant with a wave, chat, or hug for the regulars. If we had dinner, coffee was invariably on the house, and when he saw Paul emerge from the changing rooms, Alex would automatically pour a glass of Grimbergen to help with the recuperation process.

Top Délice changed our perception of Aspria Royal La Rasante as a whole. What had been a somewhat impersonal club became a welcoming, family-friendly place to escape the hustle and bustle of the city.

Paul never had much of a budget to spend on his small staff. Normally when they gathered in Brussels for their annual meeting, instead of going to a fancy restaurant like the marketing, development, sales, or almost any other team at headquarters, Paul's team's night on the town was dinner at our place, with food we bought and Paul cooked. It's a wonder those poor lads remained so loyal for all those years!

A year or two before we left Brussels, we asked Top Délice to cater the dinner. We agreed on a price, a menu, and that dinner would be at 7:30 p.m. It was just before 4:00 when Alex arrived.

"Dinner's not until 7:30," we said.

"Yes, but I have to cook. Where's your kitchen?" There would be no reheating of something prepared in advance.

Alex might have been a 25-year-old kid, but he had trained as a chef and took huge pride in his work. At Top Délice, he was more front-of-house, and they had a chef and team that ran the kitchen. Alex looked at our catering event as an opportunity to get back in the kitchen, hands-on with full responsibility.

The meal was wonderful, and Paul's team finally realized what they had been subjected to on those previous occasions when they'd politely commented favourably on the food. This was something else. Alex disappeared without a mention, but the kitchen was spotless when we discovered he was gone. The leftover food fed us for days.

When the time came to leave Brussels, we had a drop-in farewell party for friends and colleagues. The decision to ask Alex and Maria to cater for us again was an easy one.

They surprised us again when Maria showed up with Zafira, one of the servers from the restaurant. We were banned from our own kitchen, food and drink flowed all evening, and although she was the lone server, Zafira made sure no glass was empty while clearing every empty plate from wherever it was set down almost before it came to rest.

Maria and Alex, a mother-and-son team from abroad, changed the entire atmosphere at one of Brussels' most upmarket membership clubs just by treating people as people and by the personal pride and care they took in their profession.

San Daniele, Brussels: Comfortable perfection

When Paul retired from Radisson, he had six diamonds on the Yes I Can! pin he proudly wore on his lapel – one for every five years of service. One year, in addition to a CEO-signed diploma and a new pin with an extra diamond, he was given a gift card for lunch at a Michelin-star restaurant. He'd been to the restaurant once for a business dinner. The food was awesome, but Paul didn't really feel comfortable there. He gave the gift card to Kirsten and said she could treat one of her friends. Kirsten and her friend had a wonderful lunch, of course, but Kirsten shared the same feeling Paul had about the experience. It wasn't snobbish or stuffy, but it did lack the personal, welcoming feel that always accompanies a great experience.

One of Kirsten's clients at Aspria in Brussels was in the gym almost every day, and over time, Kirsten got to know her fairly well. Her partner also showed up from time to time, usually around 4:00 in the afternoon, but he was always gone again by 5:30. It turned out that Stefano owned San Daniele, a Michelin-star restaurant that had been in his family for decades. They were open for lunch and dinner, so his only chance to hit the gym was after the last lunch guest left and before he had to return to prep the front of house before they opened for dinner at 7:00 p.m.

To celebrate a special occasion one year, we decided to visit San Daniele. We knew it had a Michelin star, so were slightly wary of the atmosphere, but any apprehension we had was laid to rest almost before we were seated.

Stefano guided us gracefully to our table and brought two glasses of prosecco for us to enjoy while musing over the menu.

The menu was in French and Italian. We can read menus in those languages, especially if we have our phones on and can Google Translate any uncertainties. That wasn't necessary at San Daniele.

Stefano's father, who has sadly since passed away, came to our table and happily explained every item to us in English, clearly indicating what his personal preferences were! There was no rush, no questioning our lack of language skills. We were treated like, and we truly felt like, guests in their home. As Signor Spinelli shared the stories behind the items on the menu, our mouths watered in anticipation of the delights we would be served. Stefano topped up our prosecco, and a friendly server noted our orders and confirmed that listening to Signor Spinelli would be something we would come to be grateful for when the food arrived.

Our first evening at San Daniele is the most memorable Michelin-star experience we've had. If we had to rank our top three experiences at Michelin-star restaurants, all three spots would to go San Daniele. We were once there with the friend Kirsten had taken to lunch using the gift card Paul had been given. Both she and her husband agreed that finding a better place to celebrate a special occasion would be difficult, even in Brussels, a city that boasts more than its fair share of Michelin-star restaurants.

Although we've only visited San Daniele on three occasions, the word-of-mouth advertising we heard from others over the years told us time and again that what we experienced at the small, Italian, fine dining gem in the Ganshoren neighbourhood, on the often unexplored edge of the European capital city, was not something we experienced because we were acquainted with the owner. It was something we experienced because the owner and the entire team treat every guest like they treated us. They make people feel like they're guests in a home.

Before we moved to Canada, we did a mini tour of Europe. We started in Oslo, revisiting the hotel where Paul's career began. Our next stop was Copenhagen, the city where we met. On this final visit before we moved, we were treated like royalty at the Royal Hotel, the "world's first designer hotel" and the first hotel in the chain that has since become the Radisson Hotel Group. Upon returning to Brussels, we had one final night in the city we'd called home for a decade. Deciding where to spend that final evening was easy. We dined at San Daniele and said a fond farewell to Stefano and the team before getting a short night's sleep and embarking on our journey to our new homeland.

What have you learned? What can you do?	
1	Recognition and personalizing your service are foundations of a turnaround process.
2	Even a challenging clientele responds to human hospitality.
3	If your product is perfection, it will still benefit from human hospitality.
4	No matter how high-end the product, guests can and should feel at home, welcome, and worthy.

- Think back to some of your fine dining experiences. Which experiences stand out from the others for reasons other than the food?
- Have you ever been made to feel like a VIP guest at a fine dining restaurant? If so, what can you learn from this experience?

Franchise: Creating a Personal Touch at Scale

In the plethora of "how to build a business" books that are available, there is inevitably at least one section on how to scale your business. Scaling up quickly to great numbers through franchising and other licensing agreements may be both desirable and achievable – and the good news is, in the hospitality business, it doesn't need to happen at the cost of providing a personal touch.

The key to achieving this is probably found not so much in the corporate, cookie-cutter machine, loyalty program, or booking engines. It is found in the franchise owners, outlet managers, supervisors, and frontline shift workers' day-to-day behaviour. One of the most gratifying things about working in hospitality is that, no matter who you are or what your work function is, you have an opportunity to make a difference and create experiences that will become memorable moments for guests.

Hertz: Pink cars and the personal touch

When Paul lived in Norway, he couldn't afford a car. When we lived in Denmark, we could afford a car, but there was no place to park near our central Copenhagen apartment, and everything we needed was only a short walk away.

Several of the hotels Paul worked for had Hertz car rental offices, so whenever we needed a car, we rented from Hertz. We rented them regularly for weekend trips, and when our daughter spent two years at a school five hours' drive away, we needed cars even more often. On holiday, whether travelling to somewhere remote like Bushman's Kloof or through the mountains en route to visit Paul's parents in Kelowna, it was a pretty safe bet that if we needed a car, it would come from Hertz.

To make bookings easy, Paul had a Hertz #1 club card. At some point, we can't remember when, Paul received a letter informing him that thanks to his loyalty, he was "promoted" to the Hertz Five Star club. That promotion made booking even easier, and it also gifted us an automatic upgrade (based on availability, etc.).

In the US, one of the things we liked was that we could just choose any car in the Five Star member lot. No queue, no paperwork, no hassle. In Seattle, we once chose an almost-new car for our journey up to Canada. At the border crossing, the agent asked whose car we were driving.

"Hertz," we replied.

"Go to secondary screening," he said.

We sat in the secondary screening area while border agents checked the car for contraband, people being smuggled, or (probably) illegal drugs or weapons.

An agent returned to us in the waiting room and asked, "Who told you to take this car?"

"No one," we replied. "We could choose any car on the lot and took this one because it was the newest."

"Here's a tip," he said. "This car has California plates. We're almost always directed to search cars with California plates. Next time choose a car with plates from Washington state. It'll probably be a smoother sail through the border for you."

When exchange rates made flying into Vancouver less expensive than Seattle, more of our Canadian holidays started there than south of the border. We still booked via Hertz though, and after one of our first bookings, something happened that hadn't happened before.

After handing the car in and flying home to Europe, we received the customary survey email: "Fill out our survey and help us serve you better in the future."

Paul filled out the survey, and within minutes, he received an email from Ed, station manager for Hertz at Vancouver Airport. "Thanks for filling out the survey! Glad you were happy with the service and the car."

We're not sure if Hertz knows the value of that email Ed sent to us. It certainly cemented our loyalty to the company. And, importantly, it wasn't a one-off.

In 2015, we attended a conference in Vancouver. Before the conference started, we rented a car and explored Vancouver Island for a couple of days. We dropped the car off at the airport and took the SkyTrain downtown, where we'd be staying at Fairmont Hotel Vancouver. (This would turn out to be a lucky trip. As you'll remember from an earlier chapter, we were granted an upgrade at the hotel.)

As soon as we checked into the hotel, the survey email arrived, and almost before he'd responded to it, Paul had another email from Ed. "Glad you liked the car," it said. "Let me know next time you book."

We sent him a note saying that we already had another booking as we'd be visiting Paul's parents in the Okanagan Valley. Ed's reply was again impressively quick, and he let us know that we'd be able to enjoy a great car for our drive over the mountain passes to the interior. When we went to pick up the car, it was indeed more than a simple upgrade. It was almost brand new, and it was in one of Hertz's premium vehicle classes.

The last trip we made via Vancouver before we moved to Kelowna was for the 2017 Christmas holiday, when we'd break the big news to Paul's parents of our impending move.

When Paul booked the rental car, he sent a note to Ed to confirm that the car would be equipped with proper snow tires. Ed confirmed.

It may have changed since, but in our experience at YVR (the Vancouver airport), you didn't just collect the car off the lot as you did in Seattle. Hertz Gold and Five Star members could avoid the lines in the office and proceed to a booth in the parking lot. There's usually no waiting, but on this day, two people from abroad were in discussion with the attendant. There had been a mix-up with their booking, which they'd made for the wrong date or the wrong month or the wrong year. Still, the attendant patiently explained she would find them a car despite the busy Christmas season.

"I hope you don't mind if it's a pink car," she told them with a straight face. They got their phones out, Googled a translation of the word "pink," and responded that yes, they might mind if the car was pink. She laughed and admitted that of course the car wouldn't be pink. "Welcome to Canada!" she said as she handed over the keys to two very relieved-looking gentlemen.

When Paul stepped up to the counter and handed her his driver's license and credit card, she said, "Oh, it's you. We've been expecting you. Hope you don't mind if your car is pink and a ten-minute walk from here. It does have snow tires though, and that's what you wanted, right?" She kept an amazingly straight face for a few seconds, before saying, "Okay, so it's not pink or a ten-minute walk away. It does have snow tires though. Sometimes I do speak the truth!"

The car was a brand new Volvo XC60. It had very few kilometers on it. It had snow tires. But it also had something else.

When we opened the doors and climbed in, there was an envelope on the steering wheel. Inside was a Christmas card with a handwritten note wishing us a happy Christmas, signed by Ed and many of the staff at Hertz YVR.

We've never met Ed, but he and his staff always treated us like we're family or friends. When we handed the car in on our way back to Brussels, we stopped at the counter inside and dropped off a box of chocolates for the team. Unfortunately Ed wasn't there, but we have wonderful memories of the rental experiences we enjoyed before we moved to Canada.

Ed is proof that it's not the product, not the scalability, not the loyalty programs that differentiate customer experience between big chains. It's the people, and every person who works in hospitality has the opportunity to be that differentiator.

What have you learned? What can you do?	
1	Corporate standards are nothing without caring, professional people.
2	Small gestures can yield remarkable results.
3	An unexpected reward will be remembered.
➤ Automated surveys are statistics for corporate bean counters. What's in it for your customer if you don't have an "Ed"? Also, what's in it for you?	

Feedback and Follow-Up: Our Two Favorite F-Words

Have you ever noticed that after returning from a hotel stay, a restaurant visit, or even after getting the tires changed on your car, the business sends you a survey because "your feedback is important to them"?

Have you ever noticed that in very many cases, the email that sends you the link to the survey comes from a no-reply email address?

Have you ever wondered why, if your feedback is so important, you can't reply to them directly?

Assuming you complete the survey, how often do you get a personal response that actually addresses the feedback you gave?

Feedback is important to people. It's fully understandable that companies try to automate the process, especially in today's times when everything is data-driven and it's relatively easy to collect, collate, and analyze massive amounts of data. It's less understandable that they remove, hide, or generally make it difficult to find simple solutions for simple issues through personal contact.

Many chains have turned local guest comment cards into massive corporate data collection systems, where hotels and managers are incentivized if they have high rates of input from their guests at high average scores. This changes the focus and removes a lot of the value the guest would receive and feel if they could see that their feedback really was valued.

Automation has its place in many areas of operations, from booking to collecting guest feedback, but one needs to be careful that opportunities to provide truly exceptional service don't get lost in the process.

Automation needs to be more than data collection that can be used to optimize operation. It should be viewed as an opportunity to recognize, become better acquainted with, and make great strides towards retaining your guests.

After almost every hotel stay and often after eating at restaurants that use automated booking systems, you receive an email asking for feedback about your experience. While writing this, we had a look at our email inbox. Over 90% of the surveys received after dining in restaurants were sent from email addresses we couldn't reply to. Close to half of them sent reminders if we hadn't completed the survey within a couple of days. Interestingly, although almost every request stressed how important our feedback was for the establishments to improve their customer service, we couldn't find a single example of places that actually sent us a personal response after we completed the unsolicited survey forms. (There are only two exceptions to this rule we can think of: places where we already knew the owners or managers and Ed.)

It was also interesting to note that many of the surveys stressed that if we had any issue accessing the survey or completing a question, we should contact the survey partner, not the establishment where we had dined.

Feedback is a form of communication. Good communication runs two ways to ensure messages are properly received and understood. Good communication is also key to opening great opportunities for customer retention and word-of-mouth marketing.

That is why our second favourite F-word is follow-up. Follow-up doesn't mean that the automated survey system spits out an email saying thank you and assuring the customer that their feedback points will be addressed with the relevant parts of the operation. Follow-up means personal communication that truly shows an appreciation for the feedback received and strives to ensure the customer is satisfied with what has or will be done.

This holds true even for positive feedback. For example: "Your room attendant was delighted to hear that you noticed and appreciated that she followed up on the note you left and replaced the decaf coffee with regular."

Follow-up is also an opportunity to retain or even gain a return visit. The restaurants (and hotels) we have completed survey forms for all seem to miss this opportunity. They never respond in a personal way, but they do send us email after email encouraging us to return, sometimes offering discounts, sometimes pretending that they miss us – but never proving that they know us by actually telling us why they miss us, or that they have a special on the wine we ordered last time, or that our favourite meal is back on the menu.

The Curious Café in Kelowna

We had a less-than-great experience with an online booking system for a local restaurant. They used an impressive automated booking system, and we used it to book and note that we were celebrating a special occasion. When our server arrived and introduced herself, one of her first questions was about the reason for our visit. "Are you here for a special occasion?" It was nice that the reservation had gone through, but the restaurant missed the opportunity to show true care by taking a second or two to read the comment field in their booking system.

So when we had another special occasion and were going to go to another local restaurant – the Curious Café – we were somewhat relieved that they didn't have online booking. According to their website, reservations could be made by email or phone. Having had numerous not-so-great memories from our travels of emails going unanswered and unnoticed at establishments around the world, we decided to take the chance and send an email to the "info@" address on the website. Maybe we're just suckers for punishment.

Less than 30 minutes after we sent the email, the owner responded that our reservation was confirmed. When we arrived at the restaurant, everything was ready, and we had an enjoyable evening catching up with a couple of friends.

Because we'd enjoyed our evening so much, we sent unsolicited feedback to the manager. The owner of the Curious Café responded to our email saying he was delighted to hear we'd had an enjoyable evening. He added that he would love to have us visit one of his other local restaurants. The personal touch is effective direct marketing.

Maxine DeHart: Ramada Hotel, Kelowna

When Paul grew up in Kelowna, Maxine DeHart worked in a bank across the street from a drugstore Paul's Dad worked in. When we moved to Kelowna forty years after Paul had left the city, Maxine was a city councillor, she wrote a business column in a local paper, and she was a long-service director of sales at the Ramada Hotel.

Maxine is the kind of person that everybody in town knows, but unlike some prominent personalities, Maxine takes a real personal pride in knowing everybody that knows her.

Just in case there were any issues or interruptions to our moving plans, we planned to arrive in our new hometown about a week before the scheduled closing date, when we would be given the keys to our new home. We booked a room at the Ramada for the week because we knew Maxine through Paul's parents, and it was also just a stone's throw from where we would be living.

Almost as expected, our arrival was delayed by a day due to a minor complication at customs and immigration that led to a rolling series of missed connections, and ultimately, our first night in Canada was in Vancouver instead of Kelowna. We informed the Ramada that we would arrive a day late and Maxine replied, "No problem. Let me know when you get here."

When we came to check in, there was a sign on the desk that announced we were "Guests of the Day." When we cancelled the day before, they'd changed the sign so we didn't miss out on our turn.

Shortly after we'd checked in, Maxine called and asked if everything was okay and invited us down for coffee. At breakfast every morning, she stopped by our table, often grabbing a coffee and sitting down with us.

One day, as our jetlag was grabbing hold, we decided to skip breakfast and sleep in. Around 11:00 a.m., the phone rang. Maxine hadn't seen us at breakfast and wanted to make sure we were okay.

Now you might think that Maxine treated us like this because we knew her (or at least Paul's parents had known her) for years, and if we're truthful, that's probably part of it. But on the days that she sat and had coffee with us, we noticed that she would reach out to other guests, checking up on things with them. When she did, it was very apparent from the conversations that she knew them personally, she knew what they were in town for, and she knew the events they were planning and the needs they had. If they were locals that had just come by the hotel for breakfast or a coffee, she knew what was important to them, and that's likely why we quickly came to recognize so many of the patrons in the pub and restaurant as regulars.

In a large finance-focused newspaper in Europe, we once saw an interview with a prominent hotel manager who was asked why the journalist writing the story almost never encountered hotel managers when he checked in or came to a hotel for a drink. "In the old days, the manager was always visible," the journalist said.

The hotel manager answered, "We have people for that because I have more important things to do!" He went on to mention statistics and financial and corporate reporting amongst the things that were more important than getting to know his guests and being visible for his teams.

As a columnist, councillor, and the director of sales at a 150-room hotel, Maxine has many important things to do too, but when she's at the hotel, nothing is more important than the people they host. Believe it or not, even today, three years after our move, if we haven't stopped by the hotel for a coffee, Maxine will call us every other week, just to check in and make sure all is well in our world.

Feedback and follow-up take time. Automation simplifies the data collection process and greatly amplifies the amount of data a company can collect. Unfortunately, if it removes personal feedback and follow-up in the process, it may be silently diluting the experience of guests and customers who could become loyal visitors and unpaid word-of-mouth marketers for your business.

What have you learned? What can you do?	
1	Communication is a two-way street that confirms messages are received and understood.
2	It's wrong to put the words "your feedback is important to us" when programming your system to send surveys that will collect data and information you'll never reply to.
3	Automation can help you keep track of things, but let people communicate what your computer keeps track of and handle follow-up.
4	Collecting customer feedback can be used for more than menu- and staff shift-planning. It should be used to train people to recognize and better serve your guests.
5	Feedback is more than data; it gives opportunities to open dialogue, retain customers, and drive word-of-mouth marketing.
6	Feedback without follow-up leaves many unrealized opportunities.
➤ Think about a time you were impressed by a company's follow-up. How did it make you feel? What opportunities did it lead to?	

Children Are Also Customers

The proverb "out of the mouths of babes" tells us that kids don't mince their words. Although they can make their parents cringe with embarrassment, children will often blurt out an honest opinion, truthfully and with the best intentions. Hospitality people know that children can be demanding, but thanks to their uncensored feedback, they also provide excellent learning opportunities when we view them as customers.

Travelling with children is never easy. Most restaurants and hotels are built for adults with adult tastes and experiences (unless they are resorts that cater to families). There are two age groups that can be especially vexing: eight to ten and young adults.

Children between eight and ten don't conveniently go to sleep early and have yet to develop a palate for most fancy restaurant food. They'd much rather be eating pasta and watching television in the room. They still want the company of their parents, but they are at rather loose ends in fancy dining rooms.

Young adults can be equally difficult because they are ready to be adults, and that means trying out a new level of sophistication. But, because of restrictions on drinking ages and the limits of what's allowed at 18 (or 19 or 20), they can feel self-conscious in dining situations where cocktails are a normal part of fine dining service.

How restaurant servers handle these two different needs and honor and respect the child can go a long way to making a lifelong impression.

Agadhoe Heights: Superstar service for a kid

One of the best perks of Paul's job at a global hotel company was getting paid to travel the world. Another perk was being able to tack on a weekend getaway or family vacation. A less-than-perfect perk was that he didn't always plan the timing of the trips, and sometimes the timing wasn't great.

Shortly before Easter 2001, the call came in. Paul had to go to Galway, Ireland, to help a hotel. The trip would take place during Easter week, which is a school holiday in Denmark.

Turning the uncontrollable obstacle into an opportunity, we made a family holiday out of it. When Paul's work finished on Thursday, the hotel general manager told us he had the perfect place for us to spend the first night of our road trip around the Irish coast. He had some friends who had recently taken over management of what he described as a nice countryside hotel. He would call ahead, book us a room, and get us a favourable rate.

When we arrived at Agadhoe Heights, our daughter was less than impressed. It was out in the countryside. The only traffic we heard was a cowbell from a distant field. To an eleven-year-old's eyes, there was nothing to see and nothing to do. The pool was closed for cleaning, and worst of all, there was only one restaurant. It had one set menu, and none of the words on the menu were spaghetti or pizza. (We'd once spent a week in Tunisia, exploring only the restaurants that served spaghetti Bolognese...) Peering in through the door of the restaurant, we could see sparkling silver cutlery and crystal glasses.

We cleaned up for dinner and put on our best clothes. There was anxiety in the air as we entered the very quiet, very formal restaurant. Our server was what many people might call a stereotypical Irish woman in her sixties. She was very kind and polite; her demeanour didn't quite match the formality of the restaurant, but her professionalism was spot on.

Fresh, warm dinner rolls were delicately placed on the side plates with slim silver tongs. Our daughter picked hers up, took a bite, and plonked it down on the charger plate. Paul reached across and moved it to the side plate.

We're pretty sure the server witnessed the game of checkers or chess that continued throughout the three-course meal. Each time our daughter took a bite of her bun, she would place it on the charger plate, and if that spot was covered by a dinner plate, she'd just put the bread on the table. Without saying anything, Paul would reach over and move it to the side plate. As dinner progressed, what had started as a silent protest at the lack of pasta and burgers turned into a quiet game of trying not to giggle when the bread was moved.

The server remained a quiet, consummate professional throughout. She explained each course, often in ways designed to make our daughter feel comfortable. It wasn't with the fancy-schmancy jargon from the menu. It was in clear, Irish accented English with explanations like "the way my grandmother made it for me."

We had a delicious dinner. Our daughter not only behaved very well, apart from the silent game she played with Paul, but she also admitted that it had been an excellent evening. So excellent, she said, that she thought we deserved to remain seated and have a post-dinner coffee, instead of rushing back to the room so she could watch TV. (That was a discussion we often had when we travelled while our daughter was young.)

We thanked our daughter for being so considerate and, because we were in Ireland, ordered Irish coffee. Like the rest of our meal, the coffee was wonderful – Irish whiskey, excellent coffee, and no whipped cream. Whipped cream doesn't belong in Irish coffee; real Irish double cream does, and that's what we had. Since then, every Irish coffee we've had has been compared to Agadhoe Heights' Irish coffee. Most come nowhere close.

You may think that this is a good story, but not an exceptional service lesson. That's only because the lesson was still to come.

As our glasses emptied and we were getting ready to leave, our server came over with two more Irish coffees for us and a Coke for our daughter.

"You always have to have an Irish coffee in each leg, or you could be a bit wobbly when you walk out!" she said.

Our server knew that we'd had no choice but to dine in their restaurant. We'd arrived at the hotel fairly late. We were hungry and tired, and there was little chance we'd drive all the way down to Killarney to eat. She'd seen the apprehension in our eyes when we walked in, and she'd observed the bread game that had been played throughout the meal.

At even the most formal restaurants, people are people. Understanding their individual situations and needs makes a world of difference.

Mandalay Bay, Las Vegas: A minor issue of underage alcohol service

Our daughter's birthday present when she turned 18 was a trip to Las Vegas. We booked into the Mandalay Bay and were rewarded with a wonderful view of the Strip.

The few days we spent there were filled with family things: shopping in the outlet malls during the day and seeing shows in the evening. (Cirque du Soleil's *Ka* remains our favourite.)

On our last evening in the city, we went to a top-floor luxury restaurant to celebrate what in Denmark is a major milestone in a person's life. When you turn 18, everything becomes legal. You can drive, you can vote, and you can drink.

In Las Vegas, the legal drinking age is 21.

The restaurant had set menus. Each menu had a suggested wine pairing that could be added. We ordered a menu with the wine pairing for each of us.

"I'll need to see ID," the server said.

"Oh dear, we forgot our passports in our hotel on the other side of town," we lied. We're lousy liars. The server saw through us immediately.

"Sorry, I need ID," she said.

"What if I guaranteed to take the hit if there's a raid?" Paul asked.

The server looked around, asked if we were sure, and then shrugged and said, "Okay." We had a nice evening, but it only made it into this story because of another server who handled a similar situation in a completely different and, for the restaurant, both a more responsible and a more profitable manner.

Hyatt Regency, Huntington Beach: Three glasses to go

After a few days in the desert, we headed to the California coast and checked in to the Hyatt Regency Huntington Beach. It was lavish and lovely, right on the beach, and the perfect spot to spend our final few vacation days.

They also had a fantastic fine dining restaurant. When we ordered drinks, we ordered wine for the three of us.

"I'm sorry," said our server, "I'll need to see some ID from you." She addressed our daughter directly.

"I forgot it in my room," our daughter lied, just like we had done in Vegas.

"I'm sorry," said the server.

We explained that it was a big birthday. We explained that in Denmark, 18 is the legal age. We explained that in Vegas, they had been much more forthcoming.

It didn't work.

"I really need to see it. I wouldn't want to lose my job, and we wouldn't want to lose the license for the restaurant," she said. "I can only serve you wine," she said, looking at us. "If you like it, you can always order a bottle to take back to your room. You're responsible for what you do there."

We had an excellent meal, even though our daughter likely would have preferred Cabernet to Coke.

Afterwards, we did ask for a bottle to take back to the room. Our server smiled and complied, bringing us a bottle, a corkscrew, and three clean, crystal glasses.

She had remained professional throughout. She followed the rules of the restaurant and the state of California. She even sold an extra bottle of wine, and thanks to the third glass, she also received a larger tip than she otherwise could have expected.

Some say rules are meant to be broken. Others feel that they shouldn't be broken, but if you can bend them or exploit loopholes in them, then that is okay no matter what.

But rules are usually in place to protect us, to protect others, and to protect our society.

Our server was ethical, and she enforced the rules without compromising them and without compromising her or our integrity.

What have you learned? What can you do?	
1	Recognize children as individuals; respect them and respect their parents.
2	Observation without intervention. The server in Agadhoe saw our situation, let the games go on, and rewarded us afterwards.
3	Children can be demanding customers, but their honest, straightforward comments provide great learning opportunities.
4	Children aren't guests by choice. Understanding that they are customers because their parents are hungry can help you empathise with their less-than-enthusiastic behaviour.
5	Treat children as guests, using language they can relate to.
6	Rules aren't meant to be broken, and following them doesn't have to mean guests won't be happy when they leave.
7	Empathise with parents – it's not always easy for them either!

- Have you ever taken a child to a restaurant (or witnessed a child at a restaurant) and felt that the staff made the experience more pleasurable? How could their strategies in dealing with child customers relate to other areas of hospitality?

Not Picture Perfect: Resolving Problems

Despite what you may think after a few hours of scrolling through Instagram, just like life, travel and hospitality are not always a picture-perfect experience. But what can turn around a problematic travel experience is the human touch. Some problems just cannot be handled by robots and automation, and when things go wrong, a kind human can be the difference between arriving on time with your carefully selected suit or having to present at an important event in clothes you raced out to buy in an unfamiliar city under great pressure.

When companies rely too much on automation, especially as part of their complaint-handling and problem-solving programs, the result can be, in the words of one of the leaders in a company that made this mistake, Kafkaesque.

Even when automation does its job satisfactorily, there is always the opportunity to turn a simple solution into a celebrated story by proactively taking personal responsibility and stepping in to do what's right, to do what will turn a merely satisfied guest into a full-blown supporter.

Scandinavian Airlines: A series of unforced errors

In 2016, Paul was invited to moderate a panel at a summit for Chief Security Officers. The summit was held at George Lucas' Skywalker Ranch in California. With a brother and sister-in-law in the film industry, we couldn't pass up the opportunity. It was a high-level event, so we made sure our hair (and Paul's beard) was trimmed, our clothes were cleaned and pressed, and we even decided to travel a couple of days in advance just in case we encountered any delays.

We encountered delays. Our schedule had us on a one-stop hop from Brussels to San Francisco. At our stopover, we were informed that our onward flight was delayed. No problem, we thought. We went to the lounge for Star Alliance Gold members, grabbed some coffee and magazines, and waited for the promised updates. From time to time, we heard messages on the lounge PA system saying, "Would Ms./Mr. Somebody, travelling to San Francisco, please come to the desk for an update." After a few hours, we were still not Ms./Mr. Somebody, and the airline app was still showing the rescheduled departure time even though the clock on the wall had passed that hour. Paul left the lounge to check the monitors in the public departure hall area.

"Flight SK 935 to SFO – CANCELLED," they said.

Paul re-entered the lounge and asked the service attendant for an update.

"We're only helping those with onward connections from San Francisco," she said. "Go sit and wait."

We obeyed, and after another hour of nothing, Paul went back to the desk.

"We told you to wait. We're only helping those with onward connections from San Francisco. You're not going to get on a flight today. Go sit and wait."

We felt that was less-than-stellar service for someone with the airline alliance's top frequent flyer status at one of their key European hubs.

Rather than challenge the unhelpful attendant, we went to the transfer desk in the departure hall, where a friendly, empathetic customer service rep quickly took care of us.

"I don't know why they couldn't help you in the lounge," she said. "You've waited so long it's going to be a tight squeeze, but if you can run to Gate B6, you can catch a flight to Frankfurt and then run to catch a flight that will get you into San Francisco late tonight."

"Thank you!" we said. Then we ran. We caught the flight to Frankfurt, and we caught the flight to San Francisco.

Sometimes, it feels like it's just not your lucky day. Or evening. We landed safely in the City by the Bay. Our suitcases didn't.

We waited and waited by the baggage belt. Bags disappeared from the belt until there were none left. It continued to spin, and we counted the revolutions by recognizing a sticker advertising a shuttle service every time it went by. We hoped and hoped. Then the belt stopped.

We found a service counter for the airline's baggage handling service. Surprisingly, it was operated by the airline itself, and knowing that we wouldn't be dealing with a third-party agent raised our hopes.

A helpful young man greeted us there and said, "Oh yeah, we've been waiting for you. We knew your bags weren't on the flight." We didn't bother to ask why they hadn't just informed us on arrival rather than making us wait until the baggage belt stopped.

He took the description of our bags, wrote down the numbers from our baggage claim tags, and gave us the direct line number to the baggage service desk. "Call us tomorrow, and if we don't already have your bags, we'll give you a tracking number," he said.

Not the worst ending to our extra-long day, we thought as we hopped in a cab to our hotel. That would be the last time for several days that we would speak to a human from the airline.

The next morning, we called the number we had been given.

"Our desk is open from noon," a friendly robot told us. "Please call back later."

We called back later.

"Our customer service representatives are all busy," the robot said. "Please leave a message, and we will call you back shortly."

We left a message, but no one called us.

We called back in the evening when we knew the airline had flights arriving. The robot remained cheerful and friendly, but no humans were available to speak with us, so we left another message.

This continued for a couple of days. We even left a message notifying them (but probably only the robot) that we were changing hotels since the conference was about to begin.

The day before the conference, the robot was less friendly.

"The message box for this extension is full." It hung up, and we were left listening to a dial tone.

Since we'd been wearing our travel clothes and the extra change we had in our carry-on for three or four days, we went shopping. The sales were on at Macy's, as they always are, so we got great deals on two sets of conference-appropriate clothing.

The day the conference began, Paul called the baggage office.

"The message box for this extension is full." Dial tone.

The conference went well. Paul moderated a panel on how to start a corporate security program from scratch. He was probably chosen because he was old, as the panellists were at least 20–25 years younger and enthusiastically shared their experiences with the elderly moderator.

Skywalker Ranch is a beautiful area with top-notch facilities, and they produce delicious wines. They couldn't produce our bags, but the day before departure, our airline came through.

"Where are you staying?" the voice asked. "We have your suitcase."

This could have all had a happy-like ending, if not for the fact that when we checked in for our flight home, the agent gave us a snooty look and said, "You're overweight."

Okay, we were maybe not in the best physical form of our lives, but we were well within the accepted levels for a healthy BMI, so we quickly deduced that she meant our suitcase was overweight. It wasn't though, something the agent grudgingly accepted, likely as she bid farewell to the upselling bonus some companies give to staff that collect extra fees.

We were flying business class, so with the extra baggage allowance, we were well within regulation. (We also had an extra allowance from our Star Alliance status, but it was tricky enough to get the agent to check our business class booking.)

Upon returning home, we submitted a claim form for the cost of the clothing we had purchased along with the receipts.

A few weeks later we received a form letter from customer service. It did not address our personal experience, but only outlined their limited coverage of "care costs" and asked us to submit the receipts we had already submitted.

We resubmitted them. A month later, we had still not received a response. We tried to contact customer service but could only speak with robots. We tried the customer service online live chat function and had some fun with a robot there that tried to convince us it was human, but every time its menu reset, we knew that was unlikely.

Checking his LinkedIn connections, Paul reached out to the former head of communications at the airline who was now a senior advisor to the CEO. He had worked indirectly with Paul earlier in his career.

"Not even Frank Kafka could have designed such a story!" he replied. He also promised to alert a human who could deal with our case and said he'd share the story with Group Management.

Shortly thereafter, we received an email from what probably was a human. (It had both a first and last name, whereas the chatbot only had a first name.)

The letter said they would be transferring a reimbursement equivalent to the cost of the clothing we had purchased and that we should receive it within seven business days. The letter went on to say that "despite the difficulties you encountered on this occasion, we do hope to welcome you back in the future."

We never did receive an explanation or apology for all the little things that went awry, making mountains out of the molehills they could have been if properly dealt with. We did give an honourable mention to the check-in assistant who helped us rebook our flights when the lounge attendants had told us to "sit" and "stay" and prepare to spend the night in Copenhagen.

In hospitality, it is often said that when people have unpleasant experiences, they share it with more people than they do when they have a good experience. The conference delegates loved our tale and the daily updates we had about our chats with the airline robots. Some of them even checked their future flight bookings, hoping not to find our airline in their plans.

Air Canada: Above and beyond

We do like to share good examples too. Here's what happened to us when we moved from Brussels to Kelowna.

Our flight was booked on Air Canada, via Montreal and Vancouver, and we were scheduled to land in our new hometown around 8:00 p.m. on July 5, 2018.

The flight from Brussels to Montreal was on time and uneventful. Airlines can't be faulted for what happens at immigration and customs, and we should have perhaps foreseen the fact that we might be selected for secondary screening since we were moving to Canada and not just dropping in on summer holiday.

We had diligently, honestly, and correctly filled in the customs declaration card. That meant we ticked the "yes" box beside the "I/we have unaccompanied goods." A container of our household belongings was sailing the high seas and destined to arrive a couple of months after we did.

For the Customs and Border Services Agency (CBSA) officer, that was a pretty easy call, and we were sent downstairs to the secondary screening section at Montreal's Pierre Elliott Trudeau International Airport. After a brief wait, we had a nice chat with a second officer. Although he hadn't been away from home quite as long, he had a similar story to Paul. He'd grown up in the US, been on a gap year to Canada, where his ancestors were from, and decided to stay. We had a good chat, he welcomed us home, and our paperwork was all properly stamped and approved.

In the meantime, our connecting flight to Vancouver had departed and was probably over Moose Jaw, Saskatchewan, by the time we had all of our documents. The CBSA officer was empathetic and service-minded and guided us over to a transfer desk, where our flights were rebooked, this time via Toronto.

When the time came for boarding our flight, we were informed that Pearson Airport in Toronto was closed due to thunderstorms.

We had a good amount of time to connect in Toronto, so the news wasn't too unsettling. A short while later, we were allowed to board, and we had started to taxi towards the runway when the plane braked and started to turn around. The captain announced that there was a medical emergency on board, so we were returning to the gate.

After a short time at the gate, the captain announced that the person with the medical emergency was in good hands, but Pearson Airport was again closed due to the inclement weather. We could deplane and wait by the gate, but he wasn't optimistic on behalf of the people who had onward connections from Toronto. If we didn't want to take the chance, he said to talk to the gate staff.

We deplaned and told the gate staff we wouldn't be taking the flight to Toronto. They directed us to the transfer hall, at the opposite end of the terminal, where we would be assisted in finding an alternative route to Kelowna.

YUL (the airport code for Montreal) is a long and narrow terminal. As we approached the end where the Air Canada transfer desks were, we realized how many people per hour must fly between Canada's two largest cities; the lines were long. We may have been there for days if not for our good fortune of being Gold card holders with Star Alliance. That line was only an hour or so long.

By the time it was our turn, our options were quite limited. Even with the three-hour advantage the time zone change would give us, only one flight would get us to Vancouver, and it would arrive after the last flight to Kelowna had left.

"You choose," the agent said. "Fly to Vancouver, stay there, or fly to Toronto and stay there. Either way, you will get to Kelowna tomorrow."

"If we get to Vancouver, we can walk," Paul joked.

"It's too far to walk!" she exclaimed. Apparently dealing with hundreds of grumpy, stranded passengers had dampened her sense of humour.

We confirmed we would accept the Vancouver option and enquired about accommodation.

"Someone in Vancouver will help you," was the response. "I'm sorry, but we only have time to assist with flights from here."

Looking back at the never-ending queue of people behind us, we had no complaint about that.

Our flight landed in Vancouver shortly before midnight. There was no one at the gate, and the transfer and arrival desks were deserted, as was the rest of the terminal.

No worries, we thought. We can get a staff rate at the Radisson Vancouver Airport, where we had stayed many times over the years. It was our rest-and-relax favourite after a long flight. We always spent a night there before driving over the mountains to the Okanagan Valley where Kelowna lies.

There was no deal to be had at the Radisson. It was overbooked.

We had also once stayed at the Fairmont Vancouver Airport, an in-terminal hotel overlooking the runways and the mountains that surround the city. They had a few rooms left, but they were over $400.00, which would have been about $100.00 per hour of sleep since we were booked on the first flight in the morning to Kelowna.

We took it and hoped Air Canada would reimburse us.

The next morning, which seemed to arrive almost before our heads hit the pillows, we checked out of the hotel and into our flight to our new hometown. As usual, after almost anything you do or purchase these days, a satisfaction survey request landed in Paul's email inbox. It was from Air Canada and asked us to tell them about our flight.

He filled it out, highlighting the issues we had met along the way, none of which were Air Canada's fault, and all of which (perhaps except for accommodations in Vancouver) had been competently dealt with by airline customer service staff. He included the receipt from our night at the Fairmont.

Seconds later, the expected robotic response arrived, thanking us for completing the survey and promising that our response would help them improve future services.

That was that – or so we thought.

In September, a full two months later and just before we travelled to a large security conference in Las Vegas, Paul received an email from a human named Terisa at Air Canada. She apologized and said a cheque covering the cost of our night at the Fairmont was in the mail and that we would each be given a 25% rebate on the next flight we booked via Air Canada's website.

It was unexpected, it was above and beyond, it was appreciated, and it has made us loyal to Air Canada. Airlines get a lot of complaints, and like the example this chapter began with, many of them are warranted thanks to an over-reliance on robots and AI to deal with customer service. When Air Canada let a human read our feedback, we had a new tale to tell, and it was one we actually enjoyed sharing with our friends and colleagues at the conference in Las Vegas. Today, however, we would guess that more of our friends remember the older, bad experience from before our conference at Skywalker Ranch than the more recent, good one from Air Canada.

What have you learned? What can you do?	
1	The first word in AI is "artificial." Artificial = Fake. Computers don't listen or empathise. They compute.
2	When service suffers, people are usually both the problem and the solution.
3	Great hospitality can turn initial disappointment into great memories.
4	Complaints are normal. Listen to them. Learn from them.
5	Apologizing doesn't mean you're admitting fault.
6	Save your defence for court. In operations, focus on resolving issues.
7	Blame doesn't solve problems. Deal with that when you've extinguished the fire.
8	If you sweep problems under the carpet, someone will get hurt when they trip over the bump.

- Even with an automated help line, what personal touches could Scandinavian Airlines have added to solve the lost luggage problem sooner?
- Recall a time when you have had a problem with a company and they have resolved it satisfactorily. Was AI involved in the solution?

When It Goes South: Safety and Crisis Management

During Paul's career, it was common for his phone to ring at inconvenient times, such as the first dinner out on the first day of Kirsten's mother's first visit to Brussels after we'd moved from Copenhagen. Fortunately, it wasn't a crisis, just someone who needed step-by-step guidance to resolve a technical issue.

The phone could also ring in the middle of the night, as it did shortly after our daughter joined us in Brussels upon her return from a year as a high school exchange student in West Virginia. It was after 3:00 a.m. when an unfamiliar, young, panicky Danish voice called and said, "You guys have to come and collect your daughter; she can't walk!" Parents of teenagers will know how fast your thoughts race when you know your kid has been out dancing, and those are the first words you hear when your phone rings in the middle of the night! Fortunately, the next sentences were "No, no, no! It's not what you think! She really can't walk." So, again, no crisis, just a trip to the hospital emergency ward to get her gimpy knee reset.

Sometimes, though, the phone calls were of the worst possible kind. Like the one that came in just before we sat down to dinner with friends on November 9, 2005. An area vice president told Paul to turn on the TV, and when we did, the first images we saw were from the BBC showing the Radisson in Jordan's capital city which, along with two other hotels in Amman, had been attacked by terrorists.

Ten years later, we were in Washington, DC. Paul and his colleagues in the US State Department Overseas Security Advisory Council's Hotel Security Working Group had just been recognised for their contributions to OSAC at a lavish ceremony in the ballroom of the Ritz Carlton Hotel in Georgetown. Two nights later, as we were fast asleep, Paul's phone rang again. Terrorists were attacking the Radisson Blu Hotel in Bamako, Mali.

Phone calls like that are traumatic. You wish the phone hadn't rung, you wish the situation wasn't so bad, and, most of all, you wish there was something you could do to immediately fix things. You can't, and the sooner you can replace those thoughts, accept the facts, think of the plans you've made, the experience you have, and the support you can call on, the better.

In the previous chapters, we talked about the fact that sometimes bad things will happen. Sometimes, like on these two occasions, really bad things can happen.

When crises come calling, remember *The Martian*

In the movie *The Martian*, starring Matt Damon and based on a book by Andy Weir, an astronaut becomes stranded on Mars. Damon's character has the following to say about crises:

> *"At some point, everything's going to go south on you, and you're going to say, 'This is it. This is how I end.' Now, you can either accept that, or you can get to work. That's all it is. You just begin. You do the math. You solve one problem, and you solve the next one, and then the next. And if you solve enough problems, you get to come home."*

The Martian is, in fact, a really great example of how crisis management really works.

A crisis, when lives are lost or at stake, is not something an individual can solve on their own. Yes, it happens in Hollywood movies, but rarely in real life. The following points, which we will soon cover in more detail, apply:

- Leaders need to be visible.
- Leaders need to be approachable.
- Leaders need to be empathetic and honest and explain their actions. They need to give clear, actionable directions.

In *The Martian*, Matt Damon's character, Mark Warner, talks about doing the math and solving one problem at a time. We look at coping with a crisis as a circular series of questions that are asked, answered, and repeated until a solution is found.

- What happened? What facts do we know?
- What are we going to do?
- Who is going to do what?
- When do we reconvene?

There is no real room for speculation or long democratic discussions, no real room to set up a committee or do surveys about what people think. It's about gathering facts, making decisions, and solving problems one step at a time.

During COVID-19, the provincial health officer in British Columbia, Dr. Bonnie Henry, became somewhat of a heroine for the way she communicated with the public during the almost daily briefings she held together with the provincial health minister, Adrian Dix. Listening to her communicate, it was very clear from the outset that she is a leader and an expert, and she is highly trained in crisis management and leadership.

She was visible. She was approachable. She was empathetic and honest, and she explained her actions clearly with words that everyone understood. Her key messages to the general public never really varied from the outset: "Wash your hands. Don't touch your face. Stay home if you can, and if you go out, keep six feet away from others."

When she finished her briefings, which included factual numbers and often a focused message to a certain group of people – such as healthcare workers, young people, essential service workers, or families with at-risk members – the health minister would step up to the podium and reinforce the messages. His key words were "100% of the people following 100% of the guidance 100% of the time."

Although the daily "Dr. Bonnie and Minister Dix" briefings became must-see TV, and especially Dr. Bonnie gained a growing following of fans, it was clear that the good results the province had in dealing with the outbreak in the first phases of the pandemic were down to the fact that a large number of people pitched in with their own expertise and support.

The British Columbia Centre for Disease Control experts focused on getting the testing, statistics, and guidance as right as possible during a dynamic and developing situation for which, like most crises, there was limited factual knowledge and no known solution at the outset.

An invisible team wrote the scripts and came up with easy-to-learn and memorable messages like "It's not forever, but it is for now," and "Larger spaces, fewer faces."

The political leaders in the province stepped back and let the experts decide the direction. The province's premier vowed to govern and enact legislation that followed the health officer's guidance. Up until the premier surprisingly called a snap election, the opposition also stepped up to support their efforts, with the opposition health critic becoming a key partner, assisting the health minister with virtual town halls. As we said, there is less room for democracy and debate during a crisis, and probably less need for it too.

In some ways, what happened in British Columbia during the first six months of the pandemic was perhaps less surprising than what happened in other jurisdictions that had a tougher time coordinating actions and communication.

Let's look at another quote from *The Martian*:

> *"Every human being has a basic instinct: to help each other out. If a hiker gets lost in the mountains, people will coordinate a search. If a train crashes, people will line up to give blood. If an earthquake levels a city, people all*

over the world will send emergency supplies. This is so fundamentally human that it's found in every culture without exception. Yes, there are assholes who just don't care, but they're massively outnumbered by the people that do."

Kirsten experienced this firsthand while vacationing on an island in Thailand. Our eight-year-old daughter was bitten by a dog outside a café. A German guest immediately responded by pouring a drink on the dog so it loosened its grip on her. A doctor from Singapore rendered some immediate first aid and strongly recommended a tetanus shot. The local bartender made a call, and two other locals in a Jeep arrived and said they would take our daughter to a doctor. Kirsten rode with them through the jungle, worrying about our daughter and wondering where the ride along the dark, narrow road would take them. They arrived at a private house. The doctor who lived there cleaned and dressed the wound and administered the shot, and soon Kirsten and our daughter were back at their small hotel.

The guests in the bar could have looked the other way. The bar staff could have said it was our child's fault. The people with the Jeep could have said they didn't have time. The doctor could have said his surgery was closed. Kirsten could have said she didn't want to get into a Jeep with strangers and drive through the dark night. Instead, no matter who they were or where they were from, they all instinctively reacted in the same way to something they saw: a child in need of medical care.

You may wonder why in some places – and even in companies that are well-resourced and have huge internal support in the form of expertise, money, and manpower – crises are poorly managed. We believe this happens when people think as a company rather than as a human. "The company" tries to do what's best for itself, but that's unlikely to be what's best for people. Indeed, when BP was busy trying to do what was best for BP during the Deepwater Horizon oil spill, their CEO, who was a human, cried out that he wanted his life back. All humans are impacted by crisis. Therefore, it's more important to think like a human than as a company when exposed to one.

Dr. Bonnie Henry reminded the people of British Columbia of this every day when she ended every daily briefing with the words "Be kind, be calm, and be safe."

Crises are scary. They're uncomfortable. They bring forth feelings of fear, stress, and uncertainty. But as long as we accept that there's nothing we can do to prevent the crisis from happening once it has already happened, and as long as we remember to follow our human instincts and not what a pre-programmed bot tells us will be best for our company, we will be in a good place to start solving the problems that need to be solved, and other humans will help us solve them.

When the spotlight shines, don't hide in the shadows

When Paul first started in hotel security, nothing bad ever happened in the hotel. Well, "officially" nothing bad ever happened.

There were many interesting events, to say the least, especially at night. One of the last rounds the night security staff made through the 22-story property was to find the guests who had been too drunk to fit the key into the lock on the guest room door and passed out in the hallway. Security would ensure the key in their hand matched the number on the door and move the guest inside the room, sometimes without even waking them.

Guest room doors in the hotel were self-closing and self-locking. Guests who needed to use the bathroom in the middle of the night sometimes mistook the entry door for the bathroom. When the wife of a prominent author once made this mistake, she, like many before her, suddenly found herself completely naked in the corridor. Her husband was a sound sleeper. As Paul made his rounds, he could sense movement in the hallway, and he saw the door to the service area landing used by housekeeping swing shut. When he opened it, he saw a shadowy figure exit through the door on the opposite side of the landing. Guessing what had happened, Paul grabbed some sheets from the linen storage, and after a short game of hide-and-seek, the woman found the sheets Paul left in the hallway and wrapped herself in them. That ended the game, and she remained where she was. Over the radio, Paul verified the room number with the front desk and unlocked her door. There was a brief mention in the security "daily activity report" that room "NNN" had been unlocked for guest "XX," but no public spectacle about a famous author's wife running naked through the corridors of a luxury hotel. In the good old days before smartphones and social media, even if other people had seen the woman, they didn't have any way or anywhere to publish proof of their experience.

In any case, by the time the sun rose, guests awoke, and the hotel management and day duty staff arrived, all was normal. Nothing bad had happened during the night.

But in reality, bad things do happen. Sometimes, nothing really happens, but a bad review on Tripadvisor about a simple misunderstanding can lead to consequences, and tweetstorms can blow heavily against you if they're allowed to grow.

It used to be common to think that if left alone, bad news would blow over. The truth is that if you continually sweep problems under the carpet, sooner or later they become a bump big enough to trip over.

"Spin doctor" is a term used for people who specialize in framing perception of an issue or event in the hope that people might have a more favourable view or that the issue will at least have a less negative impact. It has been used for years in both private and political sectors to try to divert focus away from sensitive and potentially harmful issues.

It grew in popularity to the point where in the 1990s, having a so-called spin doctor was common for many political leaders, and becoming one was a sought-after title for media and communications consultants.

Life was simpler in the days before iPhones and Instagram.

When things go wrong today, the spotlight will shine publicly and brightly. Rather than trying to hide in the shadows, it's better to get onto the stage and ahead of the problem. Trying to put a spin on things will make you dizzier than a liar trying to prove Mark Twain wrong.

Sometimes, as a leader, you can feel like you spend all your time trying to get people to listen to your direction. That might be true during the good times, but in times of trouble, they'll suddenly look to you and say, "Now what are we going to do, boss?"

People need to know you are there, you have their backs and you will take the responsibility of leading the way to getting things back on track.

Being approachable, empathetic, and honest are further keys to leadership when the public eye is upon you, asking difficult questions about something you wished hadn't happened.

Approachable doesn't mean being available for every person who wants information, be they victims, staff members, or media representatives. It means ensuring there are communication channels available for them to get messages to you and setting time aside to provide the answers that you can.

Mark Twain is quoted as saying, "If you tell the truth, you don't have to remember anything." Parents teach kids to tell the truth. We all know that truth is important, but sometimes, even though we know that it is best to tell the truth, we try to paint a prettier, more positive picture. We hope that by doing so, people won't be too critical and will be more approving of our words. It might start out that way, but if the crystal-clear waters in the picture become muddied by the emerging reality of the situation, that approval will quickly become disapproval.

It's also easy to point fingers of blame to try to deflect or defend ourselves against the critical questions that arise. The airline that has frustrated passengers because of a wildcat strike can try to blame the union, but that doesn't get people to their destinations. The global hotel company that responds to a complaint about an injured child at one of their properties by saying that the property is a franchise will quickly fan the flames of a Facebook firestorm.

Defending your actions is best left to the legal team. As a business, it's better to explain actions with facts. If you say you're going to do something, do that something.

People will be critical and complain when things go wrong. Openness, honesty, empathy, compassion, and consistency through walking the talk might not immediately stop the complaints, but over time it builds trust and respect.

What have you learned? What can you do?	
1	A crisis has no solution until one is found. There are no certainties in a crisis until there are.
2	When a crisis hits, people will want to help. Be approachable.
3	Leave painting pretty pictures to artists. Focus on the truth.
4	Dealing with a crisis is a process, not a procedure.
5	Making guest safety and security a priority is a sales tool.
6	People are people, and all humans are impacted by crisis. Therefore, it's more important to think like a human than as a company when exposed to one.

- ➤ What was the last crisis you witnessed (maybe even in a movie)? Were you impressed with how leadership handled the crisis?
- ➤ In the crisis you just recalled, what would you do the same? What would you do differently?

Genuine Gratitude: The Glue That Holds It All Together

"Thank you for calling," the robot says. "Your call is important to us. Please listen carefully to the menu options since some information has changed."

The above has nothing to do with gratitude, and to us, when a robot says that our call is important to the business that has chosen to automate a guest service function, it is indeed thinking more about what's important to them than what may be important to the person who is calling.

This section deals with genuine gratitude – words and actions that show people that you care about them.

Job well done: Creating a culture of gratitude

In a recent podcast on hospitality, Pablo Torres interviewed Brian Gleeson. Brian is a former colleague of Paul's. He and his wife are our friends, although we mainly keep in touch these days by following each other's social media updates. It's a long way from Kelowna to Moscow, where they live.

Near the end of the interview, Pablo shares a story from when he was just starting out in hospitality. He and Brian were both working at the same hotel in Ireland. At the end of his first shift and every shift they shared thereafter, Brian thanked Pablo for a job well done. Pablo was at first shocked that someone would thank him just for doing his job, but obviously Brian's gratitude was so impactful that he still remembers it today, twenty years later. He said Brian's daily, personal thank you sent him home with a smile on his face. He saw it as an early sign of the natural hospitality leadership qualities Brian had. He was right. Brian has gone on to become one of the world's great hoteliers and was chosen Best Hotelier at the 2014 MKG Worldwide Hospitality Awards.

Creating a culture of gratitude, like Brian does, starts internally. It starts with leaders showing gratitude to their teams and to each other. In great companies, it continues throughout the organization.

When Paul started out, he worked mainly night shifts. At the end of every shift, colleagues thanked each other for their contribution to helping make the hotel safe, secure, and comfortable. One of Paul's closest colleagues, who worked with him for almost his entire 30+ year career, still said, "Thanks for your work," every time they spoke right up until Paul retired. The strong bond between them was built on loyalty and developed into a great friendship. The fact that they were both genuinely grateful for each other and their collective contributions was well known, and it made them one of the most trusted teams in the company. Other members of the team bought into the culture of gratitude. That was no doubt a key reason why there was almost no turnover in corporate security during Paul's entire tenure.

Creating a culture of gratitude starts with something as simple as saying thank you and meaning it. It has such a powerful impact that people will remember it throughout their own careers – people like Pablo, to whom we're grateful for allowing us to share the story he told on his podcast.

The problem with automating gratitude

Genuine gratitude is a statement of caring. Automated gratitude is not.

The phone call we mentioned in the introduction to this chapter or the survey email you get after a trip, hotel stay, or restaurant visit you booked online says something to the effect of, "Thanks for coming. Now please fill out our survey so we can collect more data that we can use to maximize our revenue from your and others' future visits." Okay, that's probably not even close to the real wording, but in our minds the "thank you" that the message starts with is less than sincere. It's from an automated system that has no feelings, so it can't really be sincere. Your response will likely also be handled by an automated system.

Genuine gratitude can only be shown by people.

Faking it as an introduction to get customers to fill out surveys to collect data that benefits you more than the customer is not genuine gratitude. Gratitude is about the customer.

When gratitude is feigned by an automated system, it will easily lead to frustration if the promises it makes are not kept.

When you call customer service and the automated answering service thanks you and tells you how important your call is, how do you feel 20 minutes later when you're still on hold? How do you feel a few hours later when the robot continues to thank you and claim that your call is important? How do you feel when, after navigating through an endless menu of options, you end up back at the main menu?

When gratitude is used as a hook to make you think a company cares, its meaning becomes diluted. True gratitude, on the other hand, can build powerful connections, memories, and loyalty.

La Bussola Restaurant, Kelowna: Going a step further

Our 18th wedding anniversary was on Monday, May 18, 2020, and for those of us who live in beautiful British Columbia, restaurants were still "COVID-closed" except for take out and delivery. On May 18, it was also a public holiday, and most nicer restaurants would be closed entirely.

Still, we did want to celebrate our special day on the day itself. A few days beforehand, we sent an email to a local, Italian fine dining restaurant, even though their website indicated they didn't deliver and, on our anniversary, might not even be open at all.

The owner replied almost immediately. "We can do something special for you. What are you wanting?"

The next day, the restaurant's maître d' sent us an email wishing us a happy anniversary and enquiring about our taste preferences and any allergies or dietary restrictions. They prepared a menu, and the maître d' asked what time we'd like it delivered.

We offered to pick it up since we knew they didn't do deliveries on the public holiday, but they insisted on taking care of delivery.

As the clock struck six, the doorbell rang, and a bearded, casually dressed, pleasant fellow arrived with a big box, explaining how our meal was packed inside it and ready to be enjoyed. I tried to offer him a tip, but he said he didn't accept tips.

"We're just grateful for your order," he said. "Thank you. Happy anniversary!"

The meal was fantastic and even included an extra dessert for us to enjoy with our after-dinner coffee.

It later dawned on us that the restaurant that didn't deliver and wasn't even open on the public holiday didn't recruit a driver just for us. It was the owner himself who had delivered our meal. He truly was grateful for our order, and we're pretty sure his actions didn't only impress us – it was likely also a very motivational gesture for his staff. His actions helped them understand that in trying times, showing your gratitude by going a step further for your customers is something good leaders do.

The restaurant, La Bussola, is part of a small group of local Italian-inspired eateries in our city. One of the others is The Curious Café, a place we featured in an earlier chapter – same owner, same commitment to hospitality.

Why is it easier to be grateful during trying times?

Gratitude is the glue that binds hospitality together. It can't be taken for granted. It can't be automated, and although sometimes it does, it can't become just an expression, phrase, or empty gesture.

The best part of genuine gratitude is how it makes you feel. Yes, it makes the customer feel good, and yes, it can even help drive loyalty and business, but it also does something to us personally.

This becomes especially visible during trying times like the world experienced when the COVID-19 pandemic hit; media was flooded with stories of people showing gratitude. People would bang pots and pans from their balconies to thank healthcare personnel and frontline workers. Airline crews wrote personal, handwritten notes to passengers to thank them for travelling.

It shouldn't take a crisis for us to realize that genuine gratitude is good for more than our corporate culture or personal brand. It's good for us as people in general.

When we're genuinely grateful, it makes tasks seem more worthwhile. We feel better about them and better about ourselves. We perform better, and, especially in service and hospitality, performing well is key to creating exceptional experiences for our customers.

All the places we've mentioned as positive examples of excellent hospitality businesses have one thing in common: They have always shown us their commitment to genuine gratitude.

What have you learned? What can you do?	
1	Genuine gratitude is a human thing; it can't be automated.
2	Saying thanks when you send a post-visit customer survey is polite, but it doesn't show genuine gratitude.
3	There are direct and personal benefits of showing gratitude. We feel better about ourselves, we feel more motivated, and we perform better.
4	We often feel a need to express gratitude in challenging times, but with practice, genuine gratitude can become a natural and contagious part of our everyday behaviour.
➤ Think about guests or colleagues you've interacted with recently who made you feel genuinely appreciated. How can you express more gratitude at work? In your life?	

Start Spinning the Bottles

Tactical tips towards practical progress

"The proof is in the pudding," they say. A bunch of feel-good stories about our worldwide travels is all fine and dandy, but what's in it for you if you work in hospitality or if you own or manage a hotel, restaurant, or retail space?

Is good old-fashioned personal service even possible in today's numbers-focused, increasingly automated world? In this section, we will help you evaluate where you are now, how you can take some simple steps today, and how you can focus on the longer term, sustainable success of your service culture.

By now you know a bit about Paul's background in corporate security, and those who know him well might guess what the first step will be. If you know his educational background, you'll also be expecting this section to contain a number of Socratic-style questions that will hopefully help you start spinning the bottles in your business or workplace.

Risk assessment: Where are we now?

In the world of security, success is often based on intelligence. Not intelligence in the IQ sense, but intelligence that can help you determine what threats you are facing and what the risk of them affecting you is, how the steps you have taken are working, and how the threat environment is evolving.

One thing that often happens when we're faced with challenges today is that we listen to the voices that tell us "if you just buy this" or "if you automate that," you will be more efficient, and all your problems will go away.

We are not anti-technology or automation-resistant, but as grandma used to say, there's a time and place for everything. In hospitality, we believe technology is awesome for information, marketing, and transactions, and less than awesome when it comes to service delivery and handling the unfortunate issues that crop up from time to time. (Revisit the section Not Picture Perfect: Resolving Problems on page 95 for an example of this.)

Therefore, it's a good idea to flip the "what can I buy" attitude on its head to start your risk assessment.

- What have you automated?
- Was it transaction- or service-related?
- Why did you automate it?
- What impact did automation have on your staff?
- If you knew then what you know now, would you have automated?
- What implications would there be from reversing any of these automations?
    - Financial (cost/benefit)?
    - Personnel?
    - Service delivery?

Then look at any automation plans you may be thinking about for the future and ask the same questions.

Before we begin: If you need help to organize the assessment, we've added some checklists and toolkits in the Annexes on page 129 and freely accessible on our website.

Once you've taken a new look at how automation has and will change your business, it's time to look at organizational changes. If upcoming automation allows you to reduce personnel numbers, consider:

- The time it will take for customers to adapt
- The impact automation will have on customer perception of service
- Whether personnel reduction is best or if enhanced service and revenue can offset the cost of automation by repositioning employees

In the final section of your risk assessment, have a look at how you train and develop personnel. What areas of training and development will need to be added, updated, or removed to maximize the benefits of the changes you make?

Gaps and vulnerabilities

The questions on the risk assessment are designed to help you think through the changes you have made and are planning to make. This section aims to take a closer look at what issues the assessment revealed that can have a negative impact you perhaps didn't previously consider.

Review your risk assessment with the following in mind.

Service touchpoints

Which service touchpoints (where human staff interact with human customers) have been lost? These are often called "moments of truth," a phrase that the legendary CEO of Scandinavian Airlines, Jan Carlzon, helped make famous back in the 1980s when he wrote a book with that title. Jan Carlzon was CEO when Paul started his hospitality career. Indirectly, he helped give Paul one of his first major career breaks, but that's a story we can share another time.

The moment of truth is the opportunity that arises every time a staff member is in direct contact with a customer. At each of these intersections, the interaction can enhance or reduce your reputation. Automation has reduced the number of these opportunities, and it's important to find out which ones are gone and which ones remain.

Staff reduction

In addition to removing moments of truth, automation often leads to reduced numbers of staff. Over time, we have come to view people as "resources" or "capital" or even the nondescript "FTE." We view them as numbers on a spreadsheet, and unfortunately, they lie in the cost column. It's easy to forget that they are people – people who do a job, and the more they do it, the more knowledge they acquire.

To discover the vulnerabilities staff reductions create, it's important to give some thought to more than the cost, their place in the organization, or the *number* of people that are no longer with you. It's important to ask *who* is no longer on the team, what they did, and what they knew.

It's also important to ask these questions when considering upcoming changes to your organization. What potential hidden skill sets might your team have? Think of things like languages your employees speak, the cultures they represent, and the opportunities their individual expertise could present.

Plan of action

You've assessed your decisions and plans. You've dug deeper to determine the potential pitfalls they have exposed. The question you may be asking now is a simple one: Now what?

Opportunity lies in building on your foundation, focusing on where the biggest difference can be made, and communicating your focus.

Your moments of truth may be fewer, but they are there, and they are opportunities to start twisting towards success. A good way to start is to pretend you're the customer. From the time they first become aware of your business and every time they consider using your business, when do they meet or interact with a person? Who do they interact with? What opportunities does the interaction provide for exceptional experiences to be created?

The next step in your plan is to review the knowledge and capabilities necessary for the team member at each touchpoint to make the most of the opportunities it provides. Do you need to adjust your training? What other support do they need to ensure they are equipped to make every moment magical?

A final section in your action plan needs to address what the moments of truth are for people who don't have direct interaction with your customers. Who do they interact with? Internally and externally? Again, every interaction is a moment of truth that will impact your culture and your customer service. Your IT people may not directly interact with your customers, but the systems they're responsible for do. What do you do to make them aware of the customer experience, so they can take that into account when working?

In a restaurant, your stewards may not interact directly with a customer, but their work is crucial to customer experience – for both internal customers, like the chefs and wait staff, and your paying customers, who will notice if the tableware is less than spotless. How can you include these team members so they understand the importance of the often-invisible cog they represent in the complex mechanism of the operation?

Making it happen

An old adage in crisis management says, "Avoid the perfect plan." It's a derivative of Eisenhower's famous line: "Plans are nothing, planning is everything."

You can write a good action plan. You can have detailed policies and procedures. You can have awesome training and educational programs. At the end of the day though, people are people. Not every guest or every employee will react to similar situations in the same way, so it's important that plans aren't too detailed when it comes to customer service. Once you start doing that, you've fallen into the trap of trying to predict how every person will respond at a specific moment of interaction. Plans should be frameworks, and your team needs to know they are empowered to make the decision that is the right one for the individual customer based on their perception of what will help the person experience excellent service.

Kirsten has worked as a trained massage therapist for many years. Just like every person reacts individually, the muscular tensions in every person's back are different. Some techniques teach therapists to apply the massage evenly. Ten strokes here, ten strokes there, etc. Customers get what they came for: a back massage. Kirsten's customers get individually adapted treatments. Her hands and fingers respond to the feedback from the muscles they're massaging and adapt accordingly. That's why her company in Copenhagen was so successful, and it's why so many of her clients today are repeat customers.

You can help build a culture of service internally by using stories like the ones in this book as part of the implementation of your plan. Remind yourself that it's the intent of your policies and procedures that is important, and as long as decisions are ethical, moral, and legal, there is room for everyone to think for themselves.

It can also be very valuable to involve your team in the development of their workplace and their responsibilities. When you're asking yourself the questions we mentioned earlier in this chapter, ask your colleagues and team members to ask themselves the same questions. Sometimes people feel that employees don't care, but it's surprising how much that changes when they know how their role fits into the overall picture. If they know you care, it becomes easier for them to show you they care.

A motto at The Always Care Consulting Company is "Communicate, Collaborate, Contribute." Communication is open and two-way, and collaboration allows everyone to bring their different skill sets to the table, so the overall contribution to your success truly is the sum of your collective capabilities.

Engaging with expertise

We've known diligent, hard-working leaders who have struggled. Especially during difficult times, some of them struggle because they feel the weight of the world, or at least the success of their business, rests on their own shoulders. They retreat to their offices, spend long hours and lonely nights poring over paperwork, trying to come up with ideas that can help. It's hard to think outside the box if you're locked in the dark inside it.

In the section above, we mentioned involving your colleagues and employees in the process. It's a sign of strength to show that you care about them and want them to play a part in improving the business.

Fresh perspective is often even easier if you involve people who don't have a direct stake in the actions you're considering. A good place to start is by engaging with local business groups, professional associations, or online networks of people in similar roles. When doing so, consider again our motto. Don't join the groups with the intent of getting your problems solved or finding new customers. Instead, engage with a clear intent to communicate openly, collaborate by sharing your own expertise, and contribute to the success of others. If this seems altruistic, wait until you try it. You'd be surprised how people respond and support you in unexpected ways – the road to making your business culture one of real service excellence is one you don't have to travel alone. And it can start with the spin of a bottle.

Conclusion

Hospitality: It's the people, period.

In 1997, Paul's responsibilities included managing the hotel group's affiliation with a growing number of airline loyalty programs, running the database marketing program (a forerunner to digital customer relationship marketing), and managing the centralized travel agent commission program. All that was in addition to his responsibilities as head of corporate safety and security for the growing group of hotels.

Days were long; nights and weekends weren't – especially since he worked most Saturdays and Sundays just to keep up. He tried to convince his superiors that with the rapid international expansion of the group and the evolving and growing threats, risks, and vulnerabilities, it was necessary to spend more time on safety and security; it deserved to be a full-time position.

His efforts fell on deaf ears. On the last working day of the year, he submitted his resignation to his boss in Oslo. Less than 30 minutes later, the CEO called from Brussels.

"Are you trying to put pressure on me?" he asked.

"No, sir," Paul replied, "To be honest, I've been trying to convince you all year that safety and security should be a full-time job. It appears you don't agree. Since we have different opinions on something that I believe is so important, I think one of us needs to take the consequences and resign. I'm guessing it's not going to be you?"

The CEO laughed and agreed. He accepted Paul's resignation. They had a good, long chat about many things, including why he had several very valid reasons not to accept Paul's suggestion. During that chat, they also talked about how the hotel industry and the company was changing.

"When I started, we were taught and even empowered to do whatever we could to ensure that guests were happy," Paul said. "Now, it sometimes feels as if we're more in the business of selling hotel rooms than caring for guests."

The legendary hotelier on the other end of the line fell silent before finally saying, "You don't mean that."

In the more than 20 years since that conversation, and even more so now than in 1997, it still seems to us that many hospitality businesses are all about the transaction. How fast can you make it happen, how many times can you make it happen, how few people do you need on staff to make it happen, and how much margin can you make whilst making it happen?

We love new technology and the speed and simplicity with which well-thought-out apps and websites allow us to gather information, make decisions, and complete transactions.

Despite the way some corporations treat us, in our minds and in the experiences we most fondly remember, hospitality is most definitely not all about transactions.

One of our favourite quotes is attributed to Maya Angelou, a wonderful woman and writer we were once fortunate enough to see in person at a corporate event in Las Vegas. Her words are more relevant for the hospitality industry today than perhaps at any time before:

"People will forget what you said, people will forget what you did, but people will never forget how you made them feel."

Using technology to reduce transaction time is wonderful. Empowering employees to provide exceptional experiences – experiences that create memorable moments and leave guests feeling fantastic – is what will keep customers returning, and it's what will keep staff from leaving.

Hospitality: It's the people, period.

Annexes

Risk assessment

The following questions will help determine your start line for turning your good service into an exceptional experience for your guests and customers. We strongly advise doing this as an exercise with your team. No one knows risks and opportunities in their workplace better than those on the front lines.

What formerly manual processes have we automated?

Process	
Service / Transaction	
Staff reduction (Y/N)	
Would you do the same today?	
Cost of reversal: Financial	
Cost of reversal: Staff numbers	
Benefit of reversal: Service improvements	

What manual processes are planned to be automated?

Process	
Service / Transaction	
Staff reduction (Y/N)	
Will this improve our overall service?	
Cost of implementation: Financial	
Cost of implementation: Staff numbers	
Benefits of implementation: Service improvements	

How has our organization changed?

Total numbers of staff		
Management changes	➤ Cost-saving	
	➤ Service impact	
Back of house changes	➤ Cost-saving	
	➤ Service impact	
Frontline changes	➤ Cost-saving	
	➤ Service impact	

How has automation changed our training and development needs?

Program	
Target group	
Service impact and potential benefits	
Need more	
Need less	
New need	
Discontinue	

Gaps and vulnerabilities

Touchpoints that have been lost	Importance for overall experience (high, medium, low)	Unforeseen consequences (historical knowledge loss, etc.)

Touchpoints that remain	Importance for overall experience (high, medium, low)	Potential hidden skill sets (languages, cultural understanding, service attitudes and capabilities)

Plan of action

Reduce impact of lost touchpoints	Importance for overall experience (high, medium, low)	Steps to remedy unforeseen consequences

Enhancing remaining touchpoints	Importance for overall experience (high, medium, low)	Steps to amplify hidden skill sets

Engaging with expertise

Resources	Financial cost	Other cost/ benefit (time, resources, skills, what can we contribute)
Local (chamber of commerce, business or industry associations)		
National / regional associations		
Professional organizations		
Other resources (training and educational programs)		
The Always Care Consulting Company (alwayscare.ca)		

Acknowledgements

Special thanks to Pablo Torres for allowing us to share his story of how important it was to him, on his first shift, to receive Brian Gleeson's thanks. You can listen to the podcast here:

https://torresconsulting.co.uk/en/interviewing-brian-gleeson-gm-at-radisson-blu-olympiyskiy-hotel-moscow-russia/

Although all of our stories are personal experiences, and we've not received any promotional fees or compensation for including them in the book, here's a list of the places we've mentioned. We're so grateful for the experiences they have given us!

- **Aghadoe Heights**, Killarney, Ireland – aghadoeheights.com
- **British Airways** – ba.com
- **Bushman's Kloof**, Clanwilliam, South Africa – bushmanskloof.co.za
- **La Bussola**, Kelowna, BC, Canada – labussolarestaurant.com
- **The Curious Café**, Kelowna, BC, Canada – thecurious.ca
- **Fairmont Hotel Vancouver**, Vancouver, BC, Canada – fairmont.com/hotel-vancouver/
- **Les Garnements**, Paris, France – facebook.com/Les-Garnements-127208140694806/
- **Hertz YVR**, Vancouver, BC, Canada – hertz.ca
- **Hyatt Regency**, Huntington Beach, CA, USA – hyatt.com
- **K*Rico**, New York, NY, USA – kriconyc.com
- **Radisson Hotel Group** – radissonhotels.com
- **The River Inn**, Washington, DC, USA – theriverinn.com
- **Rosemary's Restaurant** – This wonderful restaurant has closed, but our memories live on!
- **San Daniele**, Michelin-star quality served by friends Stefano and team – san-daniele.be
- **Skinny Duke's Glorious Emporium**, Kelowna, BC, Canada – skinnydukes.com

- **Top Délice**, Brussels, Belgium – topdelice.com / akt.brussels
- **Le Trappiste**, Brussels, Belgium – le-trappiste.com
- **Tullin's Café**, Oslo, Norway – tullins.no

We'd also like to thank Andy Weir, author of *The Martian*, for his great example of how crisis management really works. – andyweirauthor.com

Special thanks

The world is full of wonderful people and places. We would like to mention a few that have been especially helpful in forming our journey so far:

Paul's many former colleagues at Radisson Hotel Group, especially Kjell and Geert, who stuck by him for so many years.

Kirsten's former colleagues at Aspria Royal La Rasante in Brussels and her clients and employees at SlowMotion clinic for massage and wellness in Copenhagen.

Maxine DeHart, Kelowna Hotelier, who has made us feel so welcome in our new hometown.

Bjørn Platou, DeconX International, who met Paul on what was the first day of work for both of them, and they've been friends ever since. The best friend who became best man.

Places we return to

We could have included memorable moments from so many other wonderful hospitality businesses around the world, but here are just a few that we always try to make time for when we visit these locations:

Bremen, Germany

- **Radisson Blu Hotel, Bremen** – Our saving grace when a volcano in Iceland stopped flights all over Europe, which became our regular stopover on road trips to and from Denmark while we lived in Brussels. – radissonhotels.com
- **Bar Celona** – Fed us after midnight on that fateful first stopover in Bremen, and we revisited them every time we were there (but we only saw people dancing on the tables once!). – celona.de

Brussels, Belgium

- **Le Mucha** – Our neighbourhood gem during our decade in Brussels. Cozy inside all winter and a beautiful "hidden garden" in the warmer months. – lemucha.be

Copenhagen, Denmark

- **Café Alma** – Right around the corner from our apartment in Copenhagen. When we lived in Denmark, this was where we went when we didn't feel like cooking. Originally known to us as Gagge & Gaarde. – cafealma.dk
- **Krog's Fiskerestaurant** – We'll admit it. We never actually went there while we lived in Copenhagen, but we'd go now! It's managed by one of the "kids" who opened Gagge & Gaarde (now Café Alma) back in the day, so we know the service is superb! – krogs.dk
- **Cap Horn** – Right in the midst of Nyhavn. We took business acquaintances there when we lived in the Danish capital. After moving away, we often made it a point to enjoy an evening there when we visited our old hometown. – caphorn.dk

Dubai, United Arab Emirates

- **Park Hyatt Dubai** – Serenity defined. Grateful for how they took care of Kirsten while Paul was on a mission for a week in other parts of the Middle East. – hyatt.com
- **Radisson Blu Hotel, Dubai Deira Creek** – The first international, five-star hotel in Dubai (opened as an InterContinental). We have visited many times since Radisson began operating the hotel and love its traditional feel, views across the "creek" and the friendly staff, some of whom we've known for decades! – radissonhotels.com

Kelowna, BC, Canada

- **Hotel Eldorado** – Our home for a week in April 2018 while we were looking for a home! – hoteleldoradokelowna.com

- **Hotel Ramada** – Our home for a week in July 2018 while we were waiting for the keys to our new home! – wyndhamhotels.com
- **Creekside Pub** – It's our reward when we walk 8 kilometres from our home down the Mission Creek Greenway. If we lived closer, it would be our neighbourhood gem! – creeksidepub.ca
- **RedBird Brewing** – We've been following them since before they opened, and we've been enjoying their beer ever since we arrived in town. – redbirdbrewing.com
- **BNA Brewing & Eatery** – It's Skinny Duke's big brother (or sister maybe). Same owners; same wonderful food, drink, and service. – bnabrewing.com
- **MidTown Station** – There's no trains in Kelowna, but we are often passengers at MidTown! – midtownstn.com

Moscow, Russia

- **Radisson Collection Hotel, Moscow** – An architectural icon. Paul stayed there on his first trip to Moscow in 1993 when it was an old, tired Intourist hotel. It's amazing what dedication to detail and a few hundred million dollars can do to a place. – radissoncollection.com

Nice, France

- **Radisson Blu Hotel, Nice** – The view and the perfect promenade to walk up an appetite for and walk off dinner in town. – radissonhotels.com

Oslo, Norway

- **Feinschmecker** – The owner of this restaurant was a colleague at the start of Paul's career. He ran the fine dining restaurant; Paul was a security guard. Lars Erik went on to win awards, accolades, and a Michelin star. Many, many years later, we finally had a chance to visit.

Paul hadn't seen him for well over 20 years, but when we arrived, Lars Erik, in his chef's whites, met us at the entrance with two glasses of champagne. Unforgettable! – Feinschmecker.no

Rotterdam, Netherlands

- **Art Hotel, Rotterdam** – Our daughter suggested it after ducking in for a hot chocolate on a cold day. It's walking distance from her place and right outside a metro stop that will take you to town in 10 minutes. – arthotelrotterdam.com
- **Mio Papa, Rotterdam** – Simple, good, and always so friendly. It's in Art Hotel. – miopapa.nl

Seattle, WA, USA

- **13 Coins SeaTac** – We had so many fun times there during overnight stopovers in Seattle that we once even exited the airport and walked across the street for lunch between flights when we had a few hours to kill. – 13coins.com

Vancouver, BC, Canada

- **Bacchus Restaurant and Lounge** – Definition of a great hotel bar. You never know who or what you might see there, but the food, the drink, and the people will guarantee a memorable experience. It's in the Wedgewood Hotel. – wedgewoodhotel.com

Washington, DC, USA

- **Old Ebbitt Grill** – There's something about taking an evening stroll past the White House, rounding the corner onto 15th Street and being propelled into a classic American bar and restaurant. – ebbitt.com

About the Authors

Kirsten Moxness

Kirsten is an entrepreneur and expert in the fields of massage, wellness, and relaxation. She founded SlowMotion, a Copenhagen-based clinic for massage and wellness in 1993. During her 11 years at the helm, she helped propel massage into one of the most popular employee benefits in Denmark. Her many client companies included the largest law firm in Denmark, multinational pharmaceutical companies, and a global IT company's call center. With government ministers and members of the Danish Special Forces divers amongst her individual clients, she literally had the top legal minds and government officials in the palms of her hands as she led the way helping companies focus on wellness to improve employee health and job satisfaction simultaneously. After moving to Brussels, Belgium, with her husband, Paul, Kirsten provided massage and wellness services at Aspria Royal La Rasante, Brussels' most exclusive sports and wellness club.

Paul Moxness

Paul likes to say he had a four-decade gap year in Europe that included a 30-year career at a company that didn't want to hire him. He is recognized as one of the world's leading experts in hotel safety and security. Paul was a founding member of the OSAC Hotel Security Working Group and has contributed to multiple UN, OSCE, EU, and other public private partnership initiatives around the world. He was awarded a Carlson Fellow, the company's highest individual honour for leadership in 2014. After being named IFSEC's #1 Global Influencer in the Security Executives Category, Paul retired from Radisson Hotel Group in 2018, where he was global Vice President of Corporate Safety and Security. Although his career always involved safety and security, at Radisson he was amongst the first Europeans certified to conduct Yes I Can! service training, and over the years he also gained extensive experience in loyalty program, e-commerce, and general hotel management.

Reading Group Discussion Questions

1. What does hospitality mean to you?
2. What do you think you do well in hospitality? Having read this book, how do you feel you can improve?
3. What did you Google while reading – destinations, food, concepts?
4. What was your favorite story? Why?
5. Think about little touches like "spinning the bottle" you've done for a guest or experienced yourself. What was it? What was the guest's reaction, or how did it make you feel?
6. What are some ways you can recognize guests as individuals in your role?
7. What aspects of resolving problems for guests are you less familiar with? How can you review your organization's process, or who could you call on to help you become more confident?
8. What is one way you've seen your leaders or other team members show genuine gratitude?
9. What is one thing your company has automated (recently or in the last five years) that you could add value to by including a personal touch?
10. Do you or any of your team members/coworkers have a potential "hidden skill set"? (e.g., languages, cultural understanding, service attitudes, and capabilities)
11. In addition to automation/digitalization, what do you think might be the most impactful changes, challenges, and developments we will see in hospitality in the coming years?